Learning Difficulties in Reading and Writing:

A TEACHER'S MANUAL

Learning Difficulties in Reading and Writing:

A TEACHER'S MANUAL

Rea Reason and Rene Boote

NFER-NELSON

Published by The NFER-NELSON Publishing Company Ltd.,
Darville House, 2 Oxford Road East, Windsor, Berkshire SL4 1DF

First published 1986
Reprinted 1986, 1987
© 1986 Rea Reason and Rene Boote

Library of Congress Cataloging in Publication data

Reason, Rea.
    Learning difficulties in reading and writing.

    Bibliography: p.
    1. Reading – Remedial teaching. 2. Penmanship – Remedial teaching.
    3. English language – Orthography and spelling. I. Boote, Rene. II. Title.

LB1050.5.R44   1986   372.4'3   86-8394
ISBN 0-7005-1072-9

Printed and bound in Great Britain by Dotesios (Printers) Limited, Bradford-on-Avon, Wiltshire

ISBN 0 7005 1072 9
Code 8250 02 1

Contents

5. Rehearsal and repetition

6. Step-by-step teaching

7. The use of phonics at Stage I and Stage II

List of Tables

Preface

Teachers and parents want to know in concrete terms what to do about learning difficulties in reading and writing. Our aim has been to translate theoretical viewpoints into practical suggestions which can be followed by all. We have based the manual on an instructional framework which embraces both systematic practice of subskills and interactive approaches to reading. Because we have assumed that different children learn to read in different ways, the importance of providing links between the teaching methods has been stressed. The purpose has been to enable teachers to help children with specific learning difficulties to build on all aspects of reading and writing in a relaxed and encouraging manner.

The original shorter version of the manual was developed in the context of in-service training for teachers. During the past few years we have modified the content on the basis of teachers' opinions and practices, and we have evaluated these approaches by following up the progress of selected pupils. A more detailed account of these studies has been provided elsewhere (Reason, 1986).

The manual started as a collection of ideas that emerged from our own experience as teachers of pupils with specific learning difficulties. To these were added suggestions made by many teachers, in particular, members of the Stockport Reading Service, to whom we are very grateful. We are especially indebted to Muriel Bridge and Angela White at the Leicestershire Literacy Support Service for allowing us to use materials written by them. Our thanks are due to Geoffrey Roberts and to Peter Farrell, both at Manchester University, whose detailed advice helped us adapt the initial version for publication. And most of all we want to thank the many pupils, teachers and parents who have followed the suggestions and have found them useful.

The examples in the manual are based on actual case studies, most of them boys. This may reflect the imbalance between sexes among children with learning difficulties. We have wished our writing to avoid the clumsiness of referring to the child as 's/he' or 'her/him'. We have therefore assigned gender arbitrarily in different cases and, for the sake of clarity, designated the teacher as belonging to the opposite sex. No sex discrimination is intended or implied by our adoption of these conventions.

To help teachers and parents follow the suggestions presented here, we have agreed with the publishers that the alphabet cards on pages 60–62 and our own tables, record sheets and specific teaching instructions may be reproduced for individual use.

Rea Reason and Rene Boote
July 1986

Use of Copyright Material

Collins Educational Publishers (Glasgow) have kindly granted us permission to base the examples of worksheets on pages 27–31 on the reading scheme 'One, Two, Three and Away' by Sheila McCullagh. Teachers wishing to reproduce this material or to make up similar materials of their own should first obtain permission from Collins.

The alphabet cards on pages 60–62 and all tables may be reproduced for personal use.

Chapter 1   Introduction

The purpose of the manual

This manual has a practical rather than a theoretical orientation. It is written for teachers and parents of children with difficulties in acquiring reading and writing skills. Although suggestions are based on current research as we see it, drawing from both the area of reading and from more general psychological principles of learning, research evidence as such is rarely mentioned. The teaching ideas and activities have been derived from discussion with and advice from many colleagues, in particular specialist teachers, and from our own teaching experience. In addition we have used suggestions made by other authors whose names are listed in the Bibliography section. The result is a collection of ideas from many sources. The emphasis is on aspects such as 'mastery' learning and parent participation.

Our teaching methods are offered not as infallible prescriptions, but as suggestions which have proved successful with many children in the past. There is no guarantee that they will work with all children in all situations. Whilst theoretical knowledge of the processes involved in reading remains incomplete, it is essential to keep an open mind and to follow a 'hypothesis testing' approach, by trying out the effectiveness of a particular way of teaching for a particular pupil in a systematic way.

One very important point needs to be made at this stage. This guide is *not* an exhaustive account of teaching methods for pupils with reading and writing difficulties. It should be regarded as a kind of 'survival kit', an attempt to assemble in one place enough ideas to enable all teachers and parents to give each child some appropriate help. It is not a substitute for more extensive initial and in-service training but a complement to it. The Warnock Report (DES, 1978) and the 1981 Education Act imply that all teachers have responsibility for pupils with reading and writing difficulties. The progress of these pupils is too important to be left to the intermittent attention of 'experts' in or out of school. The suggestions have been written with the primary school child in mind but can be modified for older pupils. Only the general principles need be adhered to; detail should always be adapted to suit the teachers, the pupils and the parents involved.

Many schools have introduced methods of interactive reading which involve parents, or other fluent readers, in reading with their children. These methods, often described as 'shared reading' or 'paired reading', are based on the ideas of authors such as Frank Smith (1984) and give children the opportunity to acquire reading skills through plenty of pleasurable reading. We support these approaches wholeheartedly. Our concern in this manual is only with those children who, for one reason or another, have been unable to profit from less structured methods alone. In our experience, pupils with learning difficulties need, in addition, a more precise step-by-step programme of instruction. We do not want to diminish the importance of incidental learning through enjoyment of the content of books but to supplement it, when necessary, with more active practice of certain aspects of reading and writing skills. But, as described in later chapters, assisted reading of a wide range of books also forms an integral part of the suggestions offered here.

The nature of reading

The assumptions teachers make about the nature of reading determine their choice of teaching methods and materials. It is, therefore, necessary to state our own theoretical viewpoint. We regard reading as a complex skill in which the aim is primarily to understand the meaning of the text but which is dependent on the automatic recognition of words and elements within the words.

Presland (1982) has made a comprehensive review of research into normal learning processes involved in literacy skills. He concludes that the model of reading which is most consistent with the evidence is an interactive-compensatory one. This is based on the assumption that the reader simultaneously synthesizes information from several sources – previous experience, knowledge of grammar and meaning, visual and phonic information. When there is difficulty with one source of information, another may compensate for it. It is, for example, possible to deduce the meaning of a word from its context and, for beginners, the context can also sometimes make up for problems with visual and phonic recognition. In fluent reading, however, word recognition skills have become automatic while use of context is likely to remain central to the comprehension of what is read.

The interactive – compensatory model of reading provides the rationale for the teaching methods offered in this manual. It implies that the acquisition of reading can proceed via a number of different routes according to the cognitive make-up and the learning strategies of the individual. Assessment and intervention are therefore planned on a broad front so that the learner also has the opportunity to compensate for weaknesses with strengths. Some children, for example, are very good at making guesses on the basis of the context. This is a strength which should be built on. Others may not have discovered the strategies of intelligent guesswork and are relying on only one or two approaches to reading such as initial letters or a limited sight vocabulary of words they have previously learnt to read. These children, in turn, need to be shown how they can take advantage of word meanings and the content of the story.

Some children may have particular difficulty with visual and phonic information, i.e. they cannot easily acquire the skills of recognizing letters, letter sounds and words. As we regard these as automatic skills (similar to driving a car or playing a musical instrument well), pupils with difficulty will need much extra practice to the point of automatic mastery. For these children the use of repetitious drill may become necessary in the context of an instructional framework which also builds on other aspects of reading. The instructional framework will be described in Chapter Four and the subsequent chapters make more detailed suggestions for methods of teaching.

Definition of specific learning difficulties in reading and writing

Some children seem to learn to read almost without any teaching. They learn so easily and effortlessly that one wonders whether reading is a skill which must be taught and built up by practice. The majority of children learn to read slowly and steadily. They read aloud to their teachers and parents and commonly move from a sight vocabulary, single letter sounds and some instruction in sound blending and the use of contextual cues to being able to think out a great deal for themselves. With practice and encouragement they learn the skills of basic reading.

The children we are concerned with here tend to have much difficulty in starting to learn to read and a few seem unable to make a start at all. Those who can read a little, typically cannot remember a word which has been read for them on one line when it reappears on the next line. These children often reverse or confuse letters or whole words, or even whole phrases (e.g. d – b, u – n, saw – was, on – no) and they tend to have difficulty in keeping to the right place on the line or to the right line. Many young children also make such errors, but the ones we are concerned with do not seem to be able to get over their difficulties. In many cases these children make extensive use of contextual and language cues without sufficient back-up from knowledge of sound/symbol correspondence. For example, 'house' may be read as 'home' or, worse still, 'trees' may be read as 'wood'. The spellings of these children are often so unconventional that even they themselves cannot decipher what they have written. And, to make matters worse, many, but not all, struggle with the task of making their handwriting legible.

The extent and nature of the difficulties vary and no two children have the same pattern of problems. Where children with such difficulties appear to be quite like their friends in all other respects, teachers and parents may look for causes, whether constitutional or environmental, to explain the discrepancy. Children are described as dyslexic or as having deficient auditory or visual perception and memory. Often difficulties with rote learning, such as memorizing multiplication tables, are cited as evidence for specific memory defects. While these aspects are of theoretical importance, they do not, as such, help the teacher or the parent to decide what to teach.

The term 'specific learning difficulties' has been widely adopted to refer to these problems. The advantage of this term is that it reminds us to look at children's performance in real learning situations, to specify what the children can and cannot do with regard to the tasks of reading and writing, and to set appropriate learning targets which relate directly to that task. By following this kind of instructional framework, we can avoid the pitfalls of having to decide about the cut-off points for categories of difficulties, and teaching can be planned for every child regardless of labels. A few children will, however, progress very slowly despite the systematic help. They have, through teaching, been identified as having more serious difficulties and as requiring more extensive individual help.

Many researchers have attempted to investigate possible underlying patterns of constitutional weakness and the books by Tansley and Panckhurst (1981) and Young and Tyre (1983) provide very readable accounts of the literature to date. In general terms, however, children with specific learning difficulties can be described in the following way:

(a) Any child, regardless of ability or socio-cultural background, can experience specific difficulties.

(b) Emotional factors may play a part, but this becomes a 'chicken and egg' issue in that reading failure itself has emotional repercussions.

(c) Reading/writing difficulties can be seen to range from mild to severe. Every primary school class will have some pupils who are not learning to read or spell as easily as the majority. All these children need to be helped and most will progress as a result of good teaching and maturation. A few will need extensive additional help.

(d) The term 'developmental delay' has sometimes been used to describe these difficulties. The term has practical implications. In effect it means that the child who is not able to take full advantage of systematic teaching at the age of five will be able to do so at the age of six or seven or later. It is therefore essential that the missed opportunity at the earlier age is compensated for later by at least equally intensive and skilled teaching.

From an instructional point of view, the simplest operational definition of specific learning difficulties is the following:

The pupil with specific learning difficulties in reading and writing has very poor retention of a reading sight vocabulary and sound/symbol correspondence. Later, spelling errors tend to be unconventional because they reflect earlier reading difficulties.

The definition is made circular by implying that the only way we can identify pupils who have reading difficulties is by trying to teach them to read. This is deliberate. If we attempt to predict problems from available tests of, say, visual and auditory perception, we are likely to identify some children who have a pattern of perceptual weaknesses which indicate that there will be problems in learning to read but, subsequently, these children learn perfectly well. In other words, screening tests and checklists can be misleading if the items are not directly related to the task of learning to read. A thorough discussion of these aspects is provided by Pearson and Lindsay (1986). As the purpose of this manual is to consider remediation, we shall not here discuss identification any further. It is hoped that every child with reading, spelling or handwriting difficulties will benefit from the suggestions made in the following chapters.

Chapter 2   Motivation

Setting the scene

Nothing succeeds like success. Pupils who progress well take pride in their efforts. Their confidence in being able to complete a task brings them half-way towards doing so. They measure their adequacy against the performance of other children in their class, even when the school does not emphasize competition, and they may be judged by their peers and also by their teachers in terms of how well they keep up with their classmates. The 'pecking order' is there whether we like it or not. Children who feel successful develop a positive self-image at school which is further reinforced at home when parents are pleased with their progress.

The situation for children with learning difficulties can be the opposite. They can approach the learning task believing that they will not be able to complete it and their lack of confidence causes their performance to deteriorate even further. They become reluctant to try, they prevaricate, daydream and appear to be making little effort to learn. In the classroom they may concentrate their efforts on remaining inconspicuous whilst feeling guilty and inadequate. In time, they may rationalize their disappointment with themselves by doing their best to convince themselves and others that they do not care about educational achievement. They may cultivate an attitude of indifference or, seeking the limelight at any cost, they may become classroom clowns or manifest behaviour problems. Their concentration span is often limited because of the difficulty of the learning task and their distaste for it. At home they are likely to meet with disappointment and anxiety. The continuing lack of success at school may gradually generalize to other aspects of their personalities so that the pupils increasingly regard themselves as inferior.

Fortunately, because of the remarkable resilience of most children, the very bleak picture we have painted above rarely happens. Pupils can usually compensate for their scholastic problems by succeeding in other areas at school and at home, and social acceptability in the playground is not usually dependent on educational achievements. Some elements of our description can, however, be recognized in every pupil with learning difficulties, whether those difficulties are limited to literacy skills only, or whether they are of a more general nature.

At this point we need to examine our own feelings towards children with learning difficulties. We also take pride in success; seeing children learn and enjoy learning is proof of our success as teachers. When pupils are not responding to our efforts, we naturally feel disappointed, and their poor progress may threaten our sense of expertise as teachers. We can unwittingly convey our disappointment to the pupils and so make matters worse. Or we may seek explanations in terms of constitutional or environmental factors which label the children but which offer no constructive suggestions of what we can do to help them.

Learning difficulties, particularly in reading, cause parents very great anxiety. In our experience, parents want to help but they may feel inadequate to do so. They may see their child's failure as their own failure too. When parents try to help, their child may avoid that help in the same way as they have learnt to avoid reading and writing at school. Books are forgotten, messages lost. Parents may reveal their concern to the child even when they are trying to remain calm. For example, a girl who was avoiding reading practice with her father despite his willing offers, gave the following explanation: 'It would be all right if only my dad didn't sigh all the time as he hears me read.'

What we can do

The first action we can take is to form a team which involves the parents, the pupil and the teacher. The best starting point is an agreement by all that there is a difficulty, that nobody is to blame for the difficulty and that we can beat that difficulty by working hard together as a team. In effect this will mean that parents and pupils have a very clear idea of what to practise at home, how to do it and how to record success. It is important that a sense of mutual appreciation and trust becomes established. This cannot happen overnight. It will always involve a great deal more direct contact with parents than teachers may be used to; seeing, talking and working with parents takes time, equally for both parents and teachers. Because the teamwork is central to the child's progress, we believe the time is well spent.

As intervention is planned for the pupil along the lines outlined in the following chapters, teachers will find that many of the suggestions can be adapted for practice at home too. In addition, Chapter Eleven provides descriptions of schemes of parental participation which have been tried in many schools and which have already proved successful. All concerned need to feel that they have control over what is happening and that they are being fully consulted. If any of the communication links between the pupil, the teacher or the parent are faulty, motivation to learn and to teach will become affected. The teacher will have the knowledge of what to teach and how to teach it, but it will be his or her task to explain that information to the others.

It is obvious that pupils will need a great deal of encouragement. Areas in which they are succeeding need to be noticed and appreciated. It may be necessary to keep reminding them that we know that they are not generally stupid, lazy or careless and that we hold them in high regard as persons. It can often help to blame the task at hand, for example, to blame the obstinate sight word which will not allow itself to be remembered. We also need to recognize that learning to read or write is hard work for the pupil and that it requires intense concentration which can only be sustained for a relatively short period of time. The oft-quoted research project by Lawrence (1973) is worth mentioning here. Lawrence concentrated on the motivation and emotional needs of the poor readers. He reported gains in performance by children who received counselling to improve their self-esteem but no direct help with reading. While research has placed emphasis on emotional factors, it has certainly not denied the importance of direct teaching of reading.

In our opinion, the single most important contribution to a sense of success is to complete a task successfully. We may have to blinker ourselves to all the skills the child should have learnt in order to keep up with his or her peers. Instead we need to examine the task, in our case the skill of reading, to assess what the pupil does know so that we can plan the next step of learning in a way that will ensure its successful completion.

Chapter 3   What are we assessing?

Initial assessment

We shall assume that you have ensured that the pupil's vision and hearing have been checked. If you have any doubts about the child's ability to hear or see well, arrange for him or her to be examined by your school's Clinical Medical Officer or ask the parents to take their child to the family doctor. Sometimes previous hearing checks have indicated normal hearing but you still have the impression that the child is not hearing well at times. The child's poor response may be caused by a fluctuating hearing loss associated with catarrhal blockage and this needs re-referral for further investigation.

We also assume that you feel reasonably satisfied with the child's ability to comprehend and use the spoken word. It need not be particularly good as the vast majority of children have more language in their mother tongue than they will meet in their early reading books in that language. Of course there may be confusion about the words used to explain reading, for example, lack of differentiation between a *letter* and a *word* – Chapter Four provides a checklist for determining what teaching is needed here. A few children may have such noticeable problems with articulation, and sometimes language acquisition, that the association of spoken language with its written form is hindered. For example, if a child mispronounces the word 'lion' as 'wion' and makes many similar errors with other letter sounds, progress in learning to read can be hampered. It is possible to refer these children for speech therapy assessment through the agencies mentioned above, but if you think that the child has more marked learning difficulties or emotional problems, the child should be mentioned to the school's Educational Psychologist. In many areas there are also Literacy Support Services which provide advice and additional teaching for some children.

Although it is important to involve outside agencies when necessary, teachers should proceed with their own assessments of reading and writing skills. These can take several forms according to the purpose of the assessment and a brief description is given below of the main forms of assessment, each with their separate functions and different methods of observation.

Normative assessment

A norm-referenced test is essentially a measure of how the pupil's learning compares with the learning of others in his or her age group. The *Burt Word Reading Test*, the *Edinburgh Reading Tests* and the various standardized reading tests produced by the National Foundation for Educational Research are examples of normative testing. The norm-referenced test can be used as a periodic statistic of progress or as a rough starting point in determining which reading age referenced book in a reading scheme is likely to be appropriate for a particular pupil. However, pupils' scores on the test give us little direct information on what they can or cannot do and so it has limited value in helping us decide what they need to learn next. Thorough accounts of all types of reading tests are provided by Pumfrey (1985) or Vincent (1985).

Diagnostic assessment

The commonly used term 'diagnostic assessment' has become the source of much confusion as it refers to two distinct ways of thinking about learning difficulties. The first, derived from a medical model of diagnosis, involves seeking underlying psychological or neurological causes for problems. To distinguish it from the second approach to diagnostic assessment, we have labelled it 'diagnosis of cognitive deficit'. The second way of thinking, which is more usual within the educational setting, examines the child's responses to our initial teaching strategies so that the strategies can be modifed in the light of those responses. This approach includes methods such as miscue analysis, i.e. observation and classification of the kinds of errors made by the pupil. Below we shall discuss the merits of each approach separately.

Diagnosis of cognitive deficit

Difficulties in learning to read or write can be due to deficits in particular cognitive areas such as visual or auditory discrimination and memory. The pupils we are concerned with here are likely to have such difficulties. But, before embarking on extensive testing of these aspects, we must ask whether the test information will contribute to our knowledge of what to teach the pupil. We would argue that, by definition, pupils who have trouble remembering an initial sight vocabulary or who struggle with the learning of letter sounds have specific problems. Testing these aspects any further is only helpful for us as teachers if it forms the basis for deciding what the pupil needs to learn next. One school of thought maintains that we should give children training tasks to 'strengthen' their particular areas of deficit. For example, pupils with poor auditory sequential memory should be given practice in reciting sequences of numbers, and pupils with poor visual sequential memory should improve that memory by practice in memorizing the order of sequences of abstract symbols. To date, however, the weight of research evidence indicates that attempts to train up these underlying areas of deficit *do not* have any direct effect on reading. We would therefore argue strongly that the very limited time available to teachers for the assessment and teaching of individual pupils should be spent on examining only those skills which are directly related to the task of reading and writing. Young pupils, for example, might be asked to demonstrate whether they can match sight words visually, match written letter symbols, read their own first name, 'guess' some sight words from context when they are being read to or discriminate between initial letter sounds when playing 'I Spy' games. If they cannot complete these kinds of tasks, described in detail in later chapters, this is where the teaching should start.

Diagnosis of reading or spelling strategies

Diagnostic tests of reading and spelling assess children's performance in terms of what they can or cannot do. Publications such as Margaret Peters's *Diagnostic and Remedial Spelling Manual* (1975) show teachers how to categorize errors and assign children to levels of spelling achievement. In a similar way, Ted

Ames in *Teach Yourself to Diagnose Reading Problems* (1983) offers an exhaustive selection of non-standardized tests of specific aspects. Published materials of this sort take up much time to complete but they can be useful to work through as a self-training exercise because they help teachers to notice individual children's strengths and weaknesses in their daily reading and writing tasks.

Most teachers assess reading progress informally by listening to children read as part of the normal class routine. This is where the technique of miscue analysis becomes useful. In essence, it consists of noting exactly what the child says when reading aloud and comparing this with the original text. As a self-training exercise it can be useful to tape-record the performance and to note the deviations from the text at leisure. Eventually, jotting down the errors for subsequent analysis becomes part of the routine of hearing children read. For a detailed account of miscue analysis, Helen Arnold's book *Listening to Children Reading* (1982) is recommended. By completing the full analysis for some children, teachers can gain experience which enables them to select from the procedure those aspects which are most relevant for a particular child.

The advantage of this kind of diagnosis is that it identifies the child's reading strategies when reading a continuous text. For children who are beyond the initial stages of reading, this evidence may be a sufficient basis for planning further work and, in the next chapter and in Chapter Eight, the assessment of reading competence for the slightly more advanced pupil is based on examining reading errors and approaches. But some pupils, particularly the children who are stuck at the initial stages, need, in addition, more detailed and exact forms of observation. The following account of criterion-referenced assessment gives a brief description of such methods.

Criterion-referenced assessment

The teacher can make up a test to find out whether children are able to complete a certain task, for example, whether they are able to match ten specified sight words. The teacher might then decide that only if each child can match all ten words correctly has he shown that he is really able to complete the task. This is criterion-referenced assessment. In essence, the teacher has designed an informal method of checking whether a particular pupil can or cannot complete a task and this has involved deciding on a criterion or a standard of performance which the pupil has to reach. The aim has not been to compare the pupil's performance with that of the other children which is the purpose of norm-referenced tests. The aim has instead been to establish what the pupil can do so that it is possible to decide what that pupil needs to learn next. For example, if she failed to match all ten words correctly, the teacher would decide that the child needs to continue to learn this task. If the pupil passed the test, the teacher would move on to the next target which might be to teach the child to read the words in the context of sentences made out of the words. Again, when the teacher thought that the child had learnt to read the ten words, a test would be designed to check whether the target had really been mastered. If the task was mastered, the next target would be set and so on. It can be seen that criterion-referenced assessment is based on the assumption that every child needs to learn a certain hierarchy of reading skills which can, to some extent, be mapped out in advance. But teachers should also remember that the criterion or standard of success (e.g. all ten words read correctly) is based on an arbitrary decision made by the teacher and it can therefore, of course, be altered on the basis of our knowledge of the child.

This way of thinking is certainly not new to teachers and you are probably already thinking along these lines. For example, when a pupil has finished a reading book, the teacher may ask him or her to read a list of words taken from that book. If the pupil can read these words out of context and also answer questions about the book, the pupil is considered able to move on to the next book; if not, he or she may be given additional exercises or guided to another book of a parallel level of difficulty.

There are some published criterion-referenced tests or checklists. Jackson's Phonic Skills Tests provide a good example. The series of 11 tests are described in the handbook *Get Reading Right* (1971) and range from pre-reading level to the level commonly achieved by the 9- to 10-year-old. The results are recorded on a Phonic Skills Record Card and enable the teacher to identify the particular skills which are causing difficulty or which have not yet been learnt. The content of each of the 11 subtests is listed below as an illustration of the way criterion-referenced tests of phonic knowledge can be organized.

1. Sounds, names, initial sounds, final sounds using lower case lettering (group test).
2. Sounds, names using upper case lettering (group test).
3. Individual letters, lower case (individual test).
4. Individual letters, upper case (individual test).
5. Two and three letter words, e.g. at, on, hat, leg, pin, top.
6. Final consonant blends, e.g. nest, task, link, hand, lamp, mint.
7. Initial consonant blends, e.g. spin, plan, grip, prop, frog, step.
8. Vowel digraphs, e.g. rain, load, feet, moon, soil, out, coat.
9. Consonant digraphs, e.g. chip, shut, that, wheel, elephant.
10. Word endings, e.g. adventure, tension, famous, station.
11. Polysyllabic words, e.g. television, occasionally.

You may assume that the above sequence of tests indicates that there is an agreed order for teaching the various phonic rules. This is not the case. Most experienced teachers of reading are likely to have designed their own preferred sequences for teaching phonics and, on seeing the list above, they might not agree with the order of the 11 tests and would possibly also comment on certain omissions. This is fine. It illustrates well the need to have a very flexible approach to criterion-referenced assessment. There may not only be one right order of teaching reading skills; there may be many, depending on the judgement and preference of the teacher and the needs of the individual pupil. But although the order is not crucial, the checking of whether the pupil has mastered a particular target is.

A number of checklists and criterion-referenced tests are mentioned by Pumfrey (1985) and include other differently ordered tests of phonic skills, tests of pre-reading skills and word recognition tests based on the most commonly used words. But teachers do not have to obtain any of these tests as they can design similar tests of their own based on the teaching materials they are using. In order to test phonic skills, for example, they can use any manual which contains lists of words which illustrate phonic rules (see the bibliography section) and extract sample words from each list for their own tests of whether pupils have mastered the rule represented by particular words. Or better still, sample words can be extracted from a selection of reading schemes used in the school. We have provided examples of these kinds of tests in Chapter Eight of this manual.

A word of warning: The requirement to measure whether the child has mastered a target skill, such as the reading vocabulary of a book or a specified phonic rule, must not limit our teaching methods only to isolated drill of any of these aspects. As described in Chapter One, reading is a great deal more than the sum of isolated skills; it is an interaction of context and meaning with visual and auditory information. For example, the child may have passed the mastery test of reading out a list of examples of the 'magic e' rule, such as 'make', 'bake', 'shake', 'wake', 'take', 'rake', and then, later, fail to read the word 'rake' in the sentence 'I rake the leaves in the garden'. The child failed to read the word for two reasons: firstly, because he did not transfer the 'magic e' rule from the list to the context of 'real' reading and, secondly, perhaps because the meaning of the verb 'rake' was unknown to the child anyway.

The mainstay of learning to read must be the reading of stories and information which hold meaning and interest and which also contain reading vocabulary, including phonics, of a level appropriate for the child. Because the child with specific learning difficulties in reading does not learn word recognition skills as easily as the 'ordinary' child, mastery of word recognition cannot be left to chance. It is in this context that criterion-referenced assessment, which checks that the child has really learnt what we are teaching, becomes necessary. We may have to subdivide learning targets into very small steps and introduce a considerable amount of repetition in order to achieve success. The case study of James in Chapter Six provides an example of a very repetitive teaching plan. That chapter will also describe principles of programme planning and record keeping based on criterion-referenced assessment.

It is important to remember that learning targets for criterion-referenced assessment are only concerned with *the end point* of learning and that the end point should be stated in a limited measurable form. The teaching methods leading up to that target should remain as interesting, varied and meaningful as possible and should certainly include a great deal of reading practice which need not be at the complete mastery level.

In the next chapter we shall introduce a framework for assessment which has many criterion-referenced items. The framework will enable the teacher to assess the stage of reading competence reached by the individual pupil and the strengths and weaknesses of that child's approach to reading. Following from the assessment, subsequent chapters introduce methods of teaching which are considered appropriate for the child concerned.

Chapter 4 Finding the right level

An instructional framework

In planning intervention, the teacher's first task is to establish the approximate level of reading reached by the individual pupil. In other words, how far has the pupil progressed on the road to becoming a fluent reader? The assessment relates the observations about the pupil's competence to an instructional framework based on the model of reading described in Chapter One. The model assumes that the learner synthesizes information from several sources: previous experience, knowledge of grammar and meaning, visual and phonic information. It also assumes that these aspects interact in a way which can enable strengths to compensate for weaknesses, and it implies that the acquisition of reading will proceed in different ways according to the make-up and the strategies of the individual. For the purpose of assessment we have devised three main headings to cover the different aspects of learning:

1. CONCEPTS AND APPROACHES
2. VISUAL WORD RECOGNITION
3. PHONICS

Concepts and approaches refer to the reader's expectations about books. The good reader expects to gain meaning from the text and from each sentence within it, is able to predict the content and structure whilst reading, and knows the conventions of written English. The term 'visual word recognition' refers to the reader's constantly increasing number of words recognized automatically at sight. 'Phonics' is a global heading for the ability to work out the pronunciation of words from a knowledge of sound/symbol relationships.

Table 4.1 presents a framework for assessment and intervention and places the three main headings across the top of the page. These aspects of reading are then subdivided into four rough stages. It is assumed that children usually start at Stage I and proceed systematically to Stage IV and that, for each stage, there are skills under the three main headings which are acquired in parallel.

Children who are experiencing difficulty in learning to read may have developed one aspect at the expense of others. There may, for example, be an over-reliance on phonics or on contextual guessing so that a higher stage, say Stage III, has been reached in some areas while other aspects remain at Stage II. The purpose of the assessment is to pinpoint the level reached by the individual pupil under each of the three main headings. Then, bearing in mind that stronger areas can compensate for the weaker ones, appropriate intervention is planned which includes all the areas of learning.

The skills to be acquired under the three main headings are summarized in Table 4.1 and described in more detail in

Table 4.1:
Stages in learning to read

STAGES	CONCEPTS AND APPROACHES	VISUAL WORD RECOGNITION	PHONICS
I Pre-reading	(a) Listens to and converses about stories. (b) Understands the vocabulary of reading.	(a) Matches sight words. (b) Matches letters. (c) Points at letters or words on request.	(a) 'I Spy'. (b) Auditory sound blending. (c) Rhyming words.
II Beginning to read	Infers and anticipates from context and from global word cues including initial letter sounds.	Reads at least 100 words fluently from initial books of reading schemes.	Reads and spells: – single letter sounds – consonant-vowel-consonant-words e.g. 'cat'.
III Intermediate	Infers from context and meaning and uses phonics when necessary.	Extensive sight vocabulary from the middle sections of reading schemes.	Reads and spells: – consonant blends – consonant digraphs – vowel digraphs – silent 'e'.
IV Basic reading skills have been mastered	As in Stage III at a more complex level of syntax and meaning.	Reads all commonly used words. Has completed reading schemes.	Reads and spells more advanced phonics: – silent initial letters – longer word endings – polysyllabic words.

N.B. The items listed for each stage describe the end point of that stage.

the text. Note that we are here concerned with initial assessment and that teaching suggestions follow in further chapters of this guide. Note also that *the items listed for each stage only describe the end point of that stage.* For the sake of an easy overview, we have decided to limit the framework to four stages only, knowing that a very considerable amount of learning takes place before the end of a stage is reached. After trying out our format, teachers may wish to subdivide their own assessment into more easily attainable stages.

Stage I: Pre-reading

Concepts and approaches

(a) Does the child listen to and converse about stories read to him? Does he refer to the illustrations? Can he answer questions such as 'what do you think will happen next?' Can he re-tell the story with prompts from the teacher?

(b) Does the child understand the vocabulary we use when we talk about books? Table 4.2 gives a checklist of questions that you can ask. A simple picture book or a beginning reader is most suitable for this purpose.

Table 4.2:
Checklist of the vocabulary of reading

> 1. Show me the <u>first</u> page of the book.
> 2. Show me the <u>last</u> page of the book.
> 3. Show me the <u>top</u> of this page.
> 4. Show me the <u>bottom</u> of this page.
> 5. Show me the <u>front</u> of the book.
> 6. Show me the <u>back</u> of the book.
> 7. Where does the story begin?
> 8. Show me a <u>word</u>.
> 9. Show me the first word on this <u>line.</u>
> 10. Show me the words <u>under</u> the picture.
> 11. Show me the words <u>over</u> the picture.
> 12. The child points word by word as the teacher reads.

Visual word recognition

(a) VISUAL MATCHING OF SIGHT WORDS:
Materials: About five words from a beginning reader are written on two cards each (for example, *school, house, mum, big, is*). Up to ten words can be used with an older pupil.
Instructions: 'Match the words, find the words which are the same'. (Note that a young child may not understand the terms 'match', 'same' or 'different' and you may have to spend some time demonstrating and teaching this first.)
Standard of performance*: The child should be able to match all the words correctly.

(b) VISUAL MATCHING OF LETTERS:
Materials: About five letters are written on two cards each (for example a, s, t, p, i). Up to ten letters can be used with an older pupil.
Instructions: 'Match the letters, find the two letters which are the same.'
Standard of performance*: The child should be able to match all the letters.

(c) WORDS OR LETTERS:
Materials: Mix up the cards from (a) and (b) above.
Instructions: 'Show me a word.' 'Show me a letter.' Continue until you feel sure the child has demonstrated an understanding of the visual difference between the two. Then take one or more of the words, for example 'mum'; 'Point to each of the letters in this word'.
Standard of performance*: All correct.

Phonics

(a) AUDITORY RECOGNITION OF INITIAL LETTER SOUNDS: The 'I Spy' game. Our aim is to find out whether the child can 'hear' the first sound of the spoken word.

Materials: Set of, say, seven common objects (or pictures of objects) each starting with a different letter (for example, *car*, *doll*, *fork*, *pencil*, *book*, *soap*, *mirror*). The objects are placed on the table.

Instructions: First make sure that the child names the objects correctly. Then, 'I spy... something beginning with d'. *Always* use the letter sound *not* the alphabetic name of the letter. Follow this procedure for each of the objects, repeating some more than once, so that the child is not able to give the right answer by narrowing the choice to those objects which have not been mentioned. Now reverse roles so that the child instructs the teacher with 'I spy...' and shows that he or she can give the initial sound for each of the objects on the table.

*Standard of performance**:   The child should be able to complete the task without errors although a few slip-ups may be allowed if the child's attention span is limited.

Note that this is a criterion-referenced test for assessment purposes only. Details of how to teach auditory recognition of initial letter sounds will be given on page 48.

(b) AUDITORY SOUND BLENDING:

Instructions: The child is required to merge the separate sounds that make up a word and say the complete word. At the pre-reading stage there is no need for the child to understand the written representations of sound/symbol correspondence. The teacher says the sounds, pausing for a second between them, the child then says the complete word. A list of ten simple words is provided below. The first five consist of only two segments (e.g. st – op) and the following five have three segments (e.g. st – o – p).

1.	gar – den	6.	fl – a – g
2.	yell – ow	7.	st – i – ck
3.	st – op	8.	c – a – tch
4.	tr – ick	9.	tr – ai – n
5.	cr – ash	10.	el – e – phant

*Standard of performance**:   The child should blend at least nine of the ten words correctly.

(Teaching suggestions for auditory sound blending will be provided on page 50.)

(c) DETECTION OF RHYMES:

The ability to distinguish between rhyming and non-rhyming pairs of words usually develops at about the same time as auditory sound blending. It has been shown to be a precursor to the development of further phonic skills (Bradley and Bryant, 1983).

Materials: Collect a set of objects or pictures in rhyming pairs. Pictures are easier to find than objects but have less immediate appeal. Agree on the names of objects before starting. If, for example, the child refers to a clock as 'a watch', discard that pair of objects rather than correcting the name. Suitable pairs: ring, string; soap, rope; mug, jug;

bat, hat; clock, sock; map, cap; book, hook.

Instructions: Explain first the concept of rhyming. Use couplets from nursery rhymes to illustrate the point (e.g. 'Humpty Dumpty sat on the wall, Humpty Dumpty had a great fall – "this rhymes because wall and fall sound nearly the same".' 'Sing a song of sixpence, a pocket full of rye – "this does not rhyme; sixpence and rye do not sound at all the same".') Select three objects, for example, a ring, a hat, a piece of string. Ask the child to pick out the two objects which rhyme. If the child does not understand the instructions, i.e. the concept of rhyming, demonstrate and explain using some of the objects.

Standard of performance*: No errors in matching four pairs of objects or pictures.

(Further teaching suggestions for this item can be found on page 51.)

Stage II: The beginning reader

Note that the items for Stage II in Table 4.1 represent the end point of that stage and indicate that the child is ready to move on to Stage III. Obviously, a very considerable amount of learning will have taken place between the end of Stage I ('Pre-reading') and the end of Stage II. The teaching involved in helping the child bridge that gap will be the focus of later chapters; here we are only concerned with initial assessment.

If the child can complete the pre-reading tasks of Stage I but has not been assigned a reading book (for example using the 'Breakthrough to Literacy' Sentence Maker), you can conclude that he is at the beginning of Stage II. Only if the child has acquired some fluency in reading the first books of reading schemes can an assessment be made of whether he has reached the end of Stage II.

Concepts and approaches

As soon as the child is able to read from a book, the focus of our assessment becomes that of hearing him read. At this stage, we are particularly interested in his ability to use the content and illustrations of the story as guides. Guessing words from their context, initial letter, shape and length is quite acceptable, as the child's reading vocabulary is still limited.

Visual word recognition

The suggestion that the child should be able to read at least 100 words is only an approximation. There is no need to make a list of the words or to count them exactly. The term 'fluently' is of more importance. Here we are interested in immediate, automatic word recognition. If the child pauses to sound out the word, then he shows ability to use phonics, but the word has not become part of his 'sight vocabulary'. We need to make a distinction between words which are read immediately and effortlessly and words which continue to require more or less painstaking effort.

Sometimes the reading book assigned to the child is too difficult. He makes many mistakes, hesitates and cannot readily understand the meaning of the text. In this case you need to find an earlier book in the reading scheme to examine his level

* The standard of performance for the criterion-referenced tests has been determined arbitrarily on the basis of our experience. It can be changed according to teacher judgement.

of reading. However, the knowledge that the child has reached a level which is too difficult in a particular reading scheme is a significant indicator of his need for a more repetitive approach.

Phonics

Before checking progress, you need to know whether and to what extent the child has been taught single letter sounds and consonant – vowel – consonant words. In many cases only recognition skills have been taught which have not been linked with written representation as suggested here. It is our opinion that the child should be able to read and write the letter sounds and simple words before we can be sure that they have really been learnt.

SINGLE LETTER SOUNDS: The letters should be printed in random order on a sheet of paper (or on individual cards). The child is only required to say the letter sounds, not the alphabetical names. Some teachers believe that letter sounds and names should be taught in parallel as part of a drill procedure. This may have some advantage for the older Secondary-aged pupil, but we believe that the younger pupil will find such a procedure confusing. If the child can say the letter sounds, the sounds are then dictated in random order. (Teaching suggestions for this item will be provided on page 55.)

CONSONANT – VOWEL – CONSONANT WORDS: You can make up a short list of words, say ten words such as *cat*, *dog*, *hit*, *bed*, *rug*, *man*, *pot*, *pen*, *tin*, *bus*. The child demonstrates first the ability to read the words and the words are then dictated to him. (Teaching suggestions for this item will be provided on page 56).

Stage III and Stage IV

In essence Stage III and Stage IV are further extensions of Stage II. As the pupil's reading skills grow, there should be a decrease of guesses made on the basis of context alone and so reading and spelling accuracy normally become quite good. As at Stage II the focus of assessment should be that of hearing the child read an appropriate book.

By now it is not possible, or indeed necessary, to devise detailed criterion-referenced assessment items. While listening to the child read, we can note reading style and errors which tell us what the pupil needs to learn next. This is the approach described below and also in Chapter Eight. That chapter will, in addition, include some checklists of phonic skills for those pupils who have not learnt about phonic regularities in the context of reading practice.

Matching the book to the reader

A rough but easy way to determine the pupil's reading level in relation to published reading schemes is to administer any one reading test which gives the child's approximate reading age. That reading age can then be matched with the reading ages of books from reading schemes which are listed in publications such as the *NARE A – Z Reading List* (Atkinson and Gains, 1985. See Resources page at the back of this manual). It is advisable to allocate the reader to books which are one or two years below the tested reading age level. This will allow for inaccuracies in our data and will also ensure that the pupil can experience success in completing that first book quickly and with ease.

Assessment based on hearing the child read

As you listen to the child read, you need to ask the following questions:

(a) Despite your careful selection of the reading book, is the child still making many errors? For a particular pupil the procedure of matching reading books to measured reading ages may not be accurate enough. Therefore, the best way of ensuring that the book is appropriate is to hear the child read it.

(b) Can the pupil understand and remember what he has read? It is often possible to make judgements on the basis of the child's intonation as he reads, for example, he may pause in a way that indicates that he is reading for meaning. Questions which start with 'what', 'where', 'who', 'how', or 'why' can help you judge the child's level of comprehension. There is no need to cover up the story content as you ask these questions. The child will be able to demonstrate comprehension of the reading material by referring to the right page or section of the book in looking for an answer. It is always useful to observe how well the child can predict the content of what he is about to read from the content of previous pages ('What do you think will happen next?' 'Can you guess the ending?').

(c) Self-correction is a particularly important reading strategy. If the child makes an error which alters the meaning of the text, does he reread the sentence or the passage to spot where he went wrong or does he plough on? Ask the pupil whether the part which was misread makes sense to determine what interpretation has been given.

(d) Does the pupil read fluently until coming to an unknown word and then make wild guesses or just stop to have the word given to him? That pupil can be described as having an 'all or nothing' approach where visual word recognition skills are relatively good but the pupil's use of context and phonics are not as advanced. The reading 'profile' can be represented diagrammatically by referring to Table 4.1 (page 14). Whilst achievements under the 'Visual Word Recognition' column may have reached Stage III, the pupil's approach to reading and use of phonics may have remained at Stage I or Stage II level. An alternative model can involve good use of context and visual word recognition skills but a significant lag in the use of phonic cues.

(e) Does the pupil rely too much on phonics? This may reflect the way he has been taught or it may indicate specific difficulties in visual word recognition. Sometimes pupils develop faulty habits of sounding out every letter separately, for example, s−t−o−p rather than sto−p which will need to be corrected following suggestions made in the phonics section of this guide. In a few cases we may have to accept that the only way the pupil can learn to read is by relying heavily on phonics and context. Usually, however, the rate of repetition of commonly used words in reading should be increased until the words are read automatically. Referring again to Table 4.1, the pupils with this approach to reading can be described as having reached Stage III under the 'Phonics' and 'Reading Approach' headings while they have remained at the beginning of Stage II with regard to 'Visual Word Recognition'.

A record based on Table 4.1

In making up a record of the tasks mastered and stages reached under the three main headings in Table 4.1, it is useful to draw up a simple chart as illustrated in the case study of James on page 41 and the case study of Peter on page 111. An examination of the chart will then indicate the approximate level at which teaching should start and the relative strengths and weaknesses of the pupil's approach to reading. The teacher is then ready to decide about a plan based on the general considerations mentioned below and the more detailed suggestions in the rest of the manual.

Implications for teaching

1. If a child is aged nearly seven years or over and shows marked difficulty at Stage I (Pre-reading), referral to your local Educational Psychology Service or Literacy Support Service is recommended. While you are waiting for further assessment, however, you will want to continue to help the child as intensively as you can. You can concentrate on highly repetitive teaching of a limited number of 'sight words' in the context of sentence building, as described in the case study of James (Chapter Six), and on the early phonic activities in Chapter Seven. The increased rate of repetition and the very limited learning content is likely to result in progress at that level. And, to complement these activities, it is always important to read with and for the child (see Chapter Eleven).

2. Children below the age of seven who have difficulties at the pre-reading stage (Stage I) or who do not seem to progress beyond the beginning of Stage II also need to follow the approaches outlined above. If you continue to see little progress, referral should be considered to the services already mentioned. Your records of the systematic and repetitive way in which you have been teaching will provide invaluable information for further programme planning.

3. Children who are progressing slowly at Stage II or Stage III also need a balanced approach which builds on all aspects of reading. Detailed suggestions are provided in Chapter Five about ways of increasing rehearsal and repetition in the context of usual reading and writing activities. The teaching of phonic skills is discussed and described in Chapters Seven and Eight. Methods of involving parents or other fluent readers in shared reading are considered in Chapter Eleven. It scarcely needs to be said that all children will continue to enjoy hearing books they have chosen read aloud to them.

4. The child who has reached Stage III under visual word recognition and shows signs of an 'all or nothing' approach to reading will need to learn to make use of some phonics and, if they have not learnt to do so, to make reasonable guesses on the basis of the content of the text. These children, who possess relatively good visual word recognition skills, should take advantage of that strength as a support in learning to read unfamiliar words. This is done by using words which are firmly within their 'sight vocabulary' as examples of phonic regularities which are being taught. These familiar words then become mnemonic aids for remembering the phonic rule in question. A more detailed account of the approach will be given on page 69, Chapter Eight.

5. Plenty of reading practice at an easy reading level is the best help for the Stage III or Stage IV pupil who relies on phonical analysis too extensively. The words which the pupil can read easily and fluently will indicate the level of reading practice to start from. A few children may continue to read laboriously but make good sense of what they are reading. In our experience, their reading will become more fluent in time as long as reading practice is not discontinued.

Conclusion

You should now have established the approximate level of reading reached by the individual pupil and have recognized his particular strengths and weaknesses. The age of the pupil has scarcely been mentioned as, regardless of age, your task has been to determine what he *can* do so that you are able to plan what needs to be learned next. For example, the pupil may have completed Stage II with regard to visual word recognition but you have found that he is not sure of all the letter sounds for that stage. Therefore, while continuing with reading practice at the appropriate level, you would point out and emphasize the initial letter sounds as the child reads to you. You would also refer to Chapter Seven for suggestions of more systematic practice of those letter sounds.

Before ending this chapter, it is worth remembering that the four reading stages and the three main headings for each stage are based on rather arbitrary decisions made by us. Their purpose is to provide a framework for instruction and, as such, they are not intended to represent a comprehensive model of the complex processes involved in reading. No doubt, other authors would suggest different models, possibly including more stages and other headings. Therefore, this particular framework is only useful if it aids you in deciding how to help those pupils who are experiencing difficulty in learning to read.

Having assessed the child's approximate stage of reading under the main headings, there are three interdependent avenues of learning at the appropriate level: firstly, reading and spelling practice with built in rehearsal and repetition, secondly, the introduction of more systematic teaching of phonics for those who need it and, finally, plenty of assisted reading of books and other materials which are of interest to the child.

Chapter 5   Rehearsal and repetition

Introduction

Learning to read may be likened to climbing a mountain; there are several possible routes to the top. Some learners need to take a slow and laborious route while others are more fortunate in being able to take the quickest and steepest one. Our task is to guide the learner along the route which we think suits him or her best. As we want to make the journey as natural and enjoyable as possible, our aim should be to help the child pick up reading without artificial drills and without difficult rules whenever possible. It is therefore appropriate to think in terms of a range of intervention strategies and start with those which need the least amount of detailed planning.

The organization of the manual is based on this way of thinking. We start by assuming that the children who do not learn to read easily simply need more time to learn and, consequently, this chapter introduces methods of increased repetition in the context of usual reading and writing practice. Repeated opportunities to read a chosen book and additional experience with supplementary materials, which reinforce the learning of the vocabulary related to that book, are described. Ideally, such methods should be introduced in parallel with assisted reading of a wider range of books where the adult, usually the parent, reads the difficult words or reads 'in chorus' with the child. Chapter Eleven will describe these kinds of approaches in more detail.

Provided that books are chosen at the appropriate level, i.e. that much of the reading vocabulary is already familiar to the learner, the advantage of a more repetitive approach is that skills already mastered receive further practice while new learning takes place through increased rehearsal and repetition of the content. In addition, the pupil has the opportunity to acquire other reading skills incidentally.

However, some children will require even more detailed help. They are the children who have not made a start in learning to read or who are not progressing despite the activities in this chapter. A more structured approach is needed which specifies exactly the task to be learnt and then provides practice of that task until it is definitely mastered. This way of planning and teaching is described in the next chapter, Chapter Six.

Methods of increasing rehearsal and repetition
A. Prepared reading

Children who have experienced difficulties in learning to read are likely to associate books with failure and frustration. The teacher's first task is therefore to help them find pleasure and success in books. This is best achieved by letting the child select a 'new' book at the right level (see page 18, matching the book to the reader) and using the book in such a way that the pupil cannot fail to read it well. The following activities, based on suggestions provided by Muriel Bridge, should ensure successful reading.

Note that all activities relate to the vocabulary of the selected book.

Preparation before reading

Before the child makes an attempt to read the book, the teacher helps the child to make a 'picture search' to get an idea of the story. The teacher ensures that important cues are not overlooked and deliberately feeds in non-visual cues, for example, names of characters or particular words which will occur. This preliminary discussion is invaluable as it increases confidence in the use of language and gives the child an opportunity to 'shine' orally. This element of preparation (which with better readers will include an examination of the paragraph and chapter headings) is vital since it enhances the use of the reading cues of anticipation and prediction.

The first read

The teacher may well choose to read the story to the pupil or the group or even to the whole class. This will give the book prestige as it is clearly worth listening to. When reading the book to the individual child, the teacher occasionally pauses so that the child can supply a word or phrase where it will be obvious. For pupils with some phonic knowledge, the teacher may cover the word except for the first letter (or two letters in the case of, for example, th, ch, sh). This read-in by the teacher allows the story to be taken at the normal pace and with suitable expression; the emphasis is on what is happening in the story. This should be an enjoyable, unhurried experience.

Alternatively, the teacher may make a tape of a frequently used book, leaving time gaps for the pupil to supply the odd word as suggested above. The missing word may be faintly underlined in the child's book, or small peel-off stickers placed over all but the first one or two letters.

The second read

Teacher and pupil change roles. The pupil does the bulk of the reading but the teacher is ready to maintain the flow with a prompt where necessary. This does not mean that teachers should always prompt immediately as it is important to give the child time to look for cues or to self-correct without pressure. Errors which retain the meaning need not always be corrected.

Further reading

If the book is interesting and the children have experienced enjoyment and success, they may well wish to read it again. They may choose to read it silently to themselves or to take it home to read to parents or to someone other than their teacher. If there are younger siblings who cannot read, the story can be read to them too.

Play reading

Some books lend themselves to adaptation as play reading. Interest is further heightened by a specific purpose for this activity, for example, to make a tape or to perform to a group or the class. Children enjoy devising appropriate sound effects. They willingly undertake the amount of rehearsal necessary to perfect their part.

B. Work based on the reading book

The written and oral activities based on the reading book have a double benefit. Firstly, they release teacher time by providing semi-independent work for the children. Secondly, and even more importantly, they reinforce literacy skills by focusing activities on the limited, familiar area of the chosen book. In this way the pupils' needs for a more repetitive approach are met in the context of a story which they enjoy reading, writing and talking about.

Word strips

Word strips can be used with the child who is at the beginning of Stage II. Individual word flash cards are usually not recommended because they are likely to present children with the kind of memory task which does not allow them to take advantage of linguistic cues.

A phrase or short sentence is 'lifted' from the book. Children might like to choose the sentence. They copy this boldly onto a small strip of card. The teacher should allow about 4cm per word with the card 3cm deep. Initially the child may need help with the copying, for example, the teacher may mark off word spaces or even faintly write the words so that the child can trace over them. The child's first attempt is in pencil and this is brought to the teacher for approval. The child reads to the teacher what he or she has written on the card, now without the aid of book and picture context. The teacher suggests that the child makes the writing brighter by tracing over the words with a crayon or a felt-tip pen. This occasions another re-read when it is brought to the teacher. The child may then cut the strip into individual words, jumble and reassemble them by matching with the book, if necessary, but from memory if possible, and then re-read the sentence again.

A second sentence from the book may be treated in the same way. The task of re-sorting the words of two sentences will be more demanding. If mistakes are made, the child re-reads the phrase or the sentence while attending more carefully to whether it makes sense. The two cut up sentences should be stored in an envelope. Pairs of subsequent sentences should be kept in separate envelopes and identified clearly, for example, by using a different coloured card or felt-tip pen.

Writing and drawing activities

(a) The child may copy out the word-strip as a caption for a picture, either in an exercise book or loose-leaf folder, or a large wall picture.

(b) The child may choose a favourite part from the story book to illustrate and add a caption or a speech balloon derived from the text.

(c) The child reads and illustrates captions or speech balloons provided by the teacher. All the words should come from the reading book.

(d) This same treatment can be given to a series of incidents from the story or, indeed, the whole story. This requires quite sophisticated skills of remembering the entire story and selecting the main incidents in sequence. (This is suitable as a class activity and is appropriate at any level. The children can produce individual comic strip versions which can be shared, or a group zig-zag book can be made.)

(e) Pupils might like to imagine that they are a character in the book and rewrite part or all of the story in the first person. The children can use the book as a dictionary to look up words and phrases whenever necessary. They may have to rehearse the account orally, helped by their teacher, before they are able to write it.

(f) The pupil imagines what happens either before or after the story in the book and speaks/writes/draws the ideas.

(g) Some stories lend themselves to map making. Pupils label or make up a key for the incidents on their maps.

(h) The teacher may devise simple *work cards* using the vocabulary from the book. These should be brief and avoid emphasis on pointless detail. Easier questions may be page referenced. The cards can include the following types of activities.

– Fill in the missing word:

    (i)   with an initial letter cue
   (ii)   without the letter cue
  (iii)   when the word order is different from that in the reading book but the initial letter cue is still provided
  (iv)   as in *(iii)* but without the letter cue
   (v)   from a choice of three words taken from the text
  (vi)   from a choice of three words of similar appearance
 (vii)   from a choice of several words

– YES/NO questions.

– A list of sentences about the story some of which are 'silly', e.g. 'The sun is in the sea'. The child identifies the 'silly sentences'.

– Questions which begin with 'Who did ...?', 'Who said ...?', 'How did ...?', 'Why did ...?'.

– Page-referenced sentence completion where the wording is slightly different from that in the book.

– Questions which involve the child in making inferences such as 'You can tell that ... because ...'; 'I liked ... (the character) because ...'; 'I did not like ... (the character) because ...'; 'What would you do if ... (you were in the same situation as the character)?'.

– Lengthier assignments, for example asking the child to write a letter to one of the characters or to the author of the book. The story book could lead to a widening study of picture and reference books on any related topic or setting.

The following pages illustrate the kinds of suggestions made above. Many publishers of reading schemes also provide workbooks which utilize this approach and, according to the needs of the individual pupil, teachers can select from the published materials and supplement these activities with additional work if necessary. It can be difficult to decide how much extra practice will be needed; too much would slow down the pupil's progress while too little would result in the pupil not having learnt the required tasks well enough. In the next chapter we shall therefore outline a system of record keeping which can help the teacher make these judgements.

As the purpose of the extra practice exercises is to relate directly to the child's reading book, we have based the illustrations below on a well-known reading scheme (*Billy Blue-hat and the Duck-pond* from 'One, Two, Three and Away' by S. McCullagh, Collins). These exercises are, as such, not intended for the children; our intention is to provide a reference source for teachers when devising their own back-up materials. The examples have been made up by Christine Proctor. Please note that the copyright to One, Two, Three and Away is owned by Sheila McCullagh and permission to make work cards based on the scheme should be sought in writing from Collins.

Billy Blue-hat and the Duck-pond.

Set 1. Finish the missing words.

1. (p.1) There were three ducks on the p____.

2. (p.2) In the middle of the pond there w____

   a big w____ feather.

3. (p.3) Billy t____ to get the feather w____

   the s___.

4. (p.5) The d___-pond was n___very d___.

5. (p.15) Billy Blue-hat had m____ all o____ him.

---

6. Cross out the words that do not belong
   to the picture, like this ~~policeman~~

pond

    Johnny

ducks

    feather

rope

    house

Billy

    splash

stick

policeman

Set 2. <u>Find the missing words.</u>

1. Jennifer _____ on to the rope too, to _____ Johnny ___. (p.9)

2. They _____ and they pulled, but Billy was ___ stuck ___ in the mud. (p.11)

3. The policeman _____ to the pond to ___ to Billy _____. (p.12)

4. The policeman _____ mud all ___ him. (p.15)

<u>Match the words to the picture. Colour the picture.</u>

ducks

Billy

rope

pond

Johnny

Jennifer

Set 3. Cross out the wrong words.

1. Billy Blue-hat ⤌ stopped / looked / tried for a stick (p.3)

2. Mrs Blue-hat ran to the pond to ⤌ pull / came to / help pull Billy out. (p.10)

3. Mr Blue-hat ⤌ ran / rope / red to the pond to help (p.11)

4. There were ⤌ there / three / then ducks on the pond (p.1)

5. Billy was ⤌ stuck / splash / stick in the pond.

Set 4. Yes or No.

1. The village was in the middle of the duck-pond. ◯

2. Billy fell into the duck-pond. ◯

3. Jennifer went to get a rope. ◯

4. The ducks had mud all over them. ◯

5. The policeman fell on Billy. ◯

6. There was mud on Mrs Blue-hat. ◯

Set 5. <u>Fill in the missing words.</u>

1. The ducks were on the p____ in the

   middle of the v___.

2. The feather was t___ far a ___ for Billy

   to get ___ .

3. Johnny r___ to get a rope to p_____

   Billy o___.

4. Johnny t___ the rope to Billy and p___.

5. The p_____ ran to h___ Billy out o_____

   the pond.

Write what Mrs Blue-hat and Mr Red-hat are

saying to each other.

Mrs Blue-hat:

Mr Red-hat:

Mrs Blue-hat:

Set 6: <u>Put the right endings on the sentences.</u>

1. In the middle of the village ......
                    (p.1)

2. One day Billy Blue-hat ......
                    (p.2)

3. The feather was ......
                    (p.3)

4. He fell into ......
                    (p.4)

5. The duck-pond was ......
                    (p.5)

6. Johnny ran back ......
                    (p.7)

7. Billy was stuck fast ......
                    (p.8)

8. Mr Red-hat fell ......
                    (p.14)

<u>Endings</u>

... went by the pond.

... too far out.

... not very deep.

... in the mud.

... the duck-pond.

... there was a duck-pond.

... on the policeman.

... for a rope.

Audiovisual aids and microcomputers as a means of enhancing a repetitive approach

Audiovisual aids and microcomputers can be valuable supports in teaching children with difficulties in reading and spelling. But, since the technological innovations do not, as such, ensure that the content and methods of teaching have been properly planned, disillusionment with technical 'gimmicks' can set in once the novelty of the machine has worn off. Success will depend on ensuring that teaching is at the right level and that it is closely related to other appropriate learning. For example, many of the supplementary activities described in the earlier parts of this chapter can be introduced on microcomputers too. In this way the content of a chosen book receives further practice.

It is important to be clear about what a particular task is to achieve. If it is discussion with other pupils based, for example, on the computer programme 'Granny's Garden', then that is fine. But, if the intention is to make sure that the learner is acquiring specific skills, then a number of clear-cut targets should be established. It can be argued that record keeping of learning targets becomes the basis of sustained motivation even more when we use technical aids than when we are able to give the children individual teacher attention. The next chapter will describe principles of detailed programme planning and record keeping.

It is usual for commercially produced technical learning devices to provide immediate feedback of errors made. But this is not enough. Electronic toys designed to encourage spelling practice, for example, commonly lack any means of assessing the children's level of learning and the rate of repetition needed by them. Consequently, children can be faced with repeated negative feedback, instead of success, as they do not have sufficient opportunity to practise an appropriate and clearly defined task. It is perhaps not surprising to find that many such toys soon appear to lose their attraction.

Below we provide some suggestions for enhancing a more repetitive approach with the help of a tape recorder or a Language Master and we discuss briefly the use, to date, of computer programs for the teaching of reading and spelling.

A. The tape recorder

When children listen to taped stories they cannot make inferences from the reader's facial expressions or gestures and, therefore, we need to pay particular attention to voice quality. Recordings can be given a more intimate and chatty tone by lowering the volume and speaking quite close to the microphone and across it rather than into it. If the child is required to read with the taped story, it is necessary to adopt a recording technique which is different from normal speech. The teacher needs to speak slowly enough while retaining the phrasing of the text. Greenwood (1978) suggests that rhythm and modulation can be emphasized by reading functional words faster and stressing lexical words. This is achieved by beating a very slow rhythm and stressing those words which form the important cues on the strong beat, for example, 'There is a HOUSE – – at the END – – of the ROAD'. Reading the text in this manner, with longer pauses and heavy stresses on certain words, slows down the pace while retaining the meaning and sounding relatively natural. It can be helpful to mark the text in advance by underlining words which are to be stressed and marking the pauses.

Reading the whole story assisted by the tape recorder requires fairly advanced skills (end of Stage II or Stage III). The complete beginner will need more detailed planning, perhaps along the following lines:

(i)   A passage of the text is read slowly with exaggerated phrasing. The child follows the text with her finger.

(ii) The passage is repeated and the child this time joins in. The rhythm of reading needs to be consistent so that the child knows exactly when to start and what pace to adopt. Signal the beginning of the joint reading with the word 'ready' spoken in the same even rhythm.

(iii) Repeat the passage at a faster pace, introduced by 'now a little faster'.

(iv) Read the passage first, then ask the child to read after you – 'now you read'.

(v)   The child reads the passage alone and then once more listens to the taped version to check that she has read the words correctly.

(vi) The child is now ready to show off her achievement by reading the passage to her teacher, parent or friends. She can record her success on a record sheet with ticks or even stars.

Although initial recording of the procedure takes time, the tape can be retained for use with other children who are at the same level. In the classroom the child will be able to follow a highly repetitive programme of reading practice without taking up teacher time.

The tape recorder can be used to give instructions similar to those mentioned on page 25 for constructing work cards. The child can be instructed to find certain words or sentences in the text (given the page number) or the beginning of a sentence taken from the text can be dictated and the child is then required to supply the ending.

The very early reader (beginning of Stage II) can be given a written sentence made up of her initial sight vocabulary as in the case study of James, Chapter Six. The tape recording then instructs the child to underline or copy selected words from that sentence.

In very small portions, the phonic drills and spelling tests in later chapters can also be taped. If self-checking procedures are incorporated, the child can record his own progress towards mastery by giving himself a score for each completed 'test'.

B. The Language Master*

In essence, the Language Master is a tape recorder which uses 17-inch-long cards with tape stuck along the full length of the card. As the card is fed into the machine, rubber rollers grip the card and feed it past the tape head 'reading' the message. As the card can be written on, the child can read and hear the content simultaneously or, preferably, attempt to read the card first and then immediately check whether he has read it correctly.

For the purpose of word recognition, shorter cards of two and a half inches are sufficient. For greater flexibility of practice, it is recommended that a separate word card is attached with a paper clip to each Language Master card. When word cards and Language Master cards are clipped together, they can be used in many different ways:

(i) Auditory/visual matching. The word cards are separated from the Language Master cards and spread out on the table. As the Language Master cards are fed through the machine the pupil places them opposite the matching word cards. If the same number is written on the backs of each pair of cards, the activity can be made self-checking. At the end of the exercise the pupil turns over the cards and gives himself a score. As it is important to give the pupil a limited number of words at a time, particular sets of cards can be grouped by symbols or coloured markings.

(ii) Reading and checking. The word cards remain attached to the Language Master cards. The pupil tries to read each word and then checks by passing the card through the machine. If two pupils are at the same reading level, motivation can be increased by getting the pupils to work in pairs on a competitive basis, each pupil retaining the cards they read correctly.

(iii) If the word cards are removed, the Language Master cards can be used for dictation, the number on the back of each card preceding each written word. The numbers on the word cards can then be used for self-marking.

C. Computer programs

The microcomputer seems at first sight to be the ideal medium for drill and practice learning. As a 'teacher' it has great charisma. It is patient, impartial, consistent and tireless. Children are eager to use computers but teachers are now having some reservations, perhaps because early programs did not live up to their promise. Software is, however, increasing and improving all the time, and more teachers are learning to write or to adapt programs. For this reason, we do not offer a list of suitable programs. Instead, the following observations are intended to guide the teacher in selecting and devising programs for children with reading and writing difficulties:

(a) At present, some of the best uses of the computer are in group work with programs which involve discussion, decision making and problem solving. It is important that children with learning difficulties have full opportunity to participate in these groups and that they are not restricted only to 'drill and practice'. For the purpose of this manual, however, we shall consider only programs designed for individual needs.

(b) Remedial work is by its very nature individual and

˟ The Language Master is available from Nottingham Educational Supplies, 17 Ludlow Hill Road, West Bridgford, Nottingham NG2 6HD isolating. Solo work on the computer may compound this isolation and periods of work spent alone on computer work should therefore be brief.

(c) Drill and practice programs must be directly related to the child's learning needs. Programs with fixed data are therefore unlikely to be suitable. The teacher should be able to alter or enter data. Alternatively, although very time consuming, teachers may be able to devise their own programs or to find someone in the local authority who can help to write individual programs.

(d) Will the child be able to handle the instructions for using the program? Typing in words on the conventional keyboard can present many problems. Some programs require the use of only two or three keys, perhaps Return and Space Bar. The fewer the options for the user, however, the more limited the program is likely to be.

(e) An increasing number of programs use overlay keyboards with a restricted number of choices. For example, the *Sentence Builder (ESM)* allows 12 words for sentence making to be entered in the program and the same words to be written on the overlay keyboard. In this way the child can make up all possible sentences on the screen, in the same way as word cards have been used in the case study of James on page 38.

(f) The program's method of marking the child's responses is important. A wrong answer should not produce a more spectacular sound effect than the correct one. Graphics can distract attention from the learning content, for example, the frog which leaps each time a letter is selected correctly, diverts attention from the word to be learnt.

(g) In spelling we emphasize visual memory and correct order of letters. Programs which use Hangman type games, jumbled letters, anagrams or erroneous spellings should therefore be rejected if spelling competence is the aim of the practice. Another important aspect of spelling is speed of writing. If children quickly master the keyboard, speed need not be a problem, but some programs are slowed down because of the information to be processed. For example, where every letter correctly keyed is rewarded, the process of typing a single word can become excessively time-consuming.

(h) Programs claiming to teach pre-reading skills should be evaluated in terms of what they teach about reading. Learning to remember details of pictures on a screen may have no effect on recall of letters in words, or of words on a page.

(i) Programs with good graphics are attractive to children but they may not teach as much reading. The words which are easiest to illustrate are nouns, as in *Words – Words – Words*, verbs, as in *Podd* (both *ASK* software), and adjectives. These are high interest words which children tend to learn most easily anyway from the reading of books. The difficult structural words (pronouns, modifiers, auxiliary verbs) are impossible to illustrate and not interesting enough to retain from reading. We have a dilemma here: graphics can distract from structural words but programs without graphics are less interesting.

(j) The effectiveness of learning from computers or any other practice medium must be judged in terms of whether the skills learned are employed in 'real-life' situations, in this case in reading books and other information. To date, therefore, the most serious limitation for microcomputers is that they are not able to listen to the child and to give immediate prompts to indicate whether the child has read a word or passage correctly. Computers are only able to respond to some form of written message transmitted through the keyboard or other extensions such as overlays or lightpens. In other words, interaction with the computer consists of 'see to write' activities and it cannot respond to the 'see to say' skills which are the essence of reading. One might therefore argue that at present computer programs are most effectively written for higher order reading skills or for the purpose of detailed record keeping.

Conclusion

We consider plenty of reading practice at the appropriate level the most essential ingredient for success. A sense of failure caused by initial difficulties can so easily lead to avoidance of reading which in turn, prevents progress. By increasing opportunities for extra rehearsal and repetition we hope to retain the learner's success orientation. However, the work must be based on active learning. The pupil needs to read aloud and receive immediate feedback for correct responses and written exercises need to involve 'real' reading. The pupil will not learn to read if time is spent copying out written work passively or if a task can be completed on the basis of visual matching alone.

Chapter 6   Step-by-step teaching

Introduction

The activities described in the previous chapter are based on the assumption that increased opportunity for repetition and success, without very detailed records, is sufficient to ensure progress. But some children, either young children who have not made a real start in learning to read, or older pupils with more severe difficulties, need an even more exact approach. The approach follows the principles of criterion-referenced assessment described in Chapter Three and involves the teacher in setting very limited learning targets and ensuring that the pupil has really learnt a particular target task before moving on to the next one. The following case study of James should illustrate the approach. Note that teaching methods are as varied and as linguistically relevant as possible while the learning target is specified in a limited measurable form.

A case study of James

Learning targets definitely mastered

James was aged six and a half years and had not made any noticeable progress in learning to read. His teacher followed the assessment procedure described in Chapter Four and found that James could complete all the Stage I targets except for the 'I Spy' task. At Stage II he had no reliable sight vocabulary and could not read any of the single letter sounds.

Target objective for James

James's teacher decided to concentrate on the development of an initial sight vocabulary as her primary objective for James, although she would obviously also introduce a variety of other activities. The target objective was stated in the following way:

James will read these 12 flashcards fluently, unaided and in any order:

I	the	teacher
am	bus	big
going	stop	at
to	is	
school		

Note that the words were taken from the first pages of a well-known reading scheme but, alternatively, they could have been selected from the kinds of words James himself liked to use. It was important to include a sufficient variety of words, i.e. nouns, verbs, prepositions so that sentences could be made up from them (see Table 6.1 overleaf).

Table 6.1:
Examples of sentence building

Words	Sentences
I am going to school	'I am going to school' 'am I going to school'
the bus stop is	'I am going to the bus stop' 'the bus is going to school' 'stop the bus' 'the bus is going to stop' 'I am going to the bus' 'the bus is going to the bus stop'
teacher big at	'the teacher is going to the bus' 'the teacher is going to school' 'the teacher is going to the big bus' 'I am going to the big teacher' 'I am at school' 'the school is big' 'the big teacher is at school' 'the big bus is at the bus stop' etc. etc. until all the words have been mastered.

Record of progress and criterion of success

The words were listed in James's reading record book. Each word received a tick when James read the flashcard fluently and without any help. Ten ticks were considered the criterion, i.e. the standard, which indicated that James had mastered each of these sight words.

Record keeping as a reward

James was allowed, under supervision, to match the flashcards he had read with those in his record book and to give a tick to the words he had read correctly. James particularly enjoyed counting the ticks each word had received and introduced a competition between the words to see which word was the 'winner' by receiving ten ticks first.

Methods of teaching

(a) ***Sentence building***

The 12 words were introduced gradually, a few at a time, in an order which enabled short sentences to be made up from them. The sentences were written into a book which became James's 'reading book'. He illustrated his book and read it many times. Table 6.1 shows the order and the groupings in which the words were introduced and gives examples of the kinds of sentences James's teacher wrote. If 'Breakthrough to Literacy' materials had been in use in James's class, his teacher could have first helped him build up the sentence on the Sentence Maker (only using the specified words) before the sentence was copied into James's 'reading book'.

(b) ***Matching identical word cards***
For example matching 'is' to 'is'. This required two sets of small flashcards with the words listed above. James was always helped to read the word after completing the visual matching.

(c) ***Sorting for word shape***
The words were written on cards with different coloured pens and in different sizes. James sorted them for word shape. His teacher read the words for him and helped him to notice aspects such as word length, shape and visual differences between letters.

(d) ***Word recognition***
The 12 word cards were spread out on the table. James's teacher read out one word at a time and James picked out the word, for example, 'give me *at*', 'give me *school*'.

(e) ***The child teaches the teacher***
The word cards were spread out on the table. James read out one word at a time and his teacher had to find the word. Sometimes James's teacher made a mistake!

(f) ***The Language Master***
The words were written on Language Master blanks and recorded. James tried to read the word and then checked his response by putting the card through the machine.

(g) ***Further sentence building***
The 12 words were written each on several individual cards and James used the 'box of cards' to make up his own sentences as in (a) above.

(h) ***Empty the box game***
The box of cards from (g) was used. James could remove all those cards from the box which he read. He was then helped to read the rest of the cards so that the box ended up empty. Later, when James was able to read all the words, he was timed to see how quickly he could empty the box.

(i) ***Further games***
The 12 words were used for games such as Lotto; a fishing game which consisted of players closing their eyes to reach for a card behind a screen; the game of Pairs where the cards from (b) above were placed face down on the table and the winner collected the largest number of pairs. Note that in all games the players always had to read the words so that visual matching alone was not accepted.

(j) ***Sentence writing***
As for (a), i.e. the same 12 words, but now James was able to copy underneath the teacher's writing and so he also had his own writing book.

(k) ***Help from parents***
James often took his teacher-made 'reading book' home and read it to his parents. When James had mastered all the words in the box of cards, see (g), he took the box home to show what

he had learnt and his parents were very pleased. (James's parents also read many stories to him and with him – see Chapter Eleven.)

Teaching priorities

With only five minutes per day to spend on individual help for James, his teacher would make sure that a new sentence was written in his 'reading book', that James read and, later, wrote the sentence and that the 12 words were checked over and ticked if read without help.

The next target objective

James made good progress and reached the standard, or criterion, of mastery in about three weeks. The 12 words had been taken from the first reading book of one of the school's reading schemes. Now a further set of 12 words was selected from the same book and the procedure of sentence building and mastery learning was repeated for these words. However, the previously learnt 12 words were also included in the sentence building and sometimes mixed up with the new set of cards. In this way the linguistic content became richer while the previously learnt words continued to be rehearsed. When all the words from the first reading book had been mastered, James was given the book to read and he read it many times from cover to cover with much pleasure.

How to plan a step-by-step reading programme

The case study of James illustrates the procedure of planning a detailed programme. In more general terms, the sequence followed by James's teacher is presented diagrammatically in Table 6.2 and, to provide an overview of the planning and teaching involved, we shall discuss below each of the subheadings in Table 6.2.

Table 6.2:
Diagram of step-by-step planning

(a) ASSESS THE PUPIL'S LEVEL OF READING

(b) DECIDE ON PRIORITY TEACHING AREA(S)

(c) PLAN LEARNING STEPS

(d) CHOOSE TEACHING METHODS AND TEACH

(e) RECORD AND EVALUATE PROGRESS

(a) Assess the pupil's level of reading

The assessment follows the framework described in Chapter Four and summarized in Table 4.1 (page 14). It involves decisions about the *stage* of reading reached by the pupil and his or her relative strengths and weaknesses under the three headings of 'Concepts and Approaches', 'Visual Word Recognition', and 'Phonics'. This format of assessment is illustrated in the lengthier case study of Peter on page 111. The case study of James is presented in this way in Table 6.3.

Table 6.3:
Assessing James's reading skills

CONCEPTS AND APPROACHES	VISUAL WORD RECOGNITION	PHONICS
Stage I achieved: James listens to and converses about stories. He understands the vocabulary of reading. **Stage II** not learnt.	**Stage I** skills learnt: James matches words and letters. **Stage II:** no reliable sight vocabulary.	**Stage I:** James does not 'pass' the 'I Spy' test but he shows that he has the phonic skills required by the other two tests. **Stage II** not started.

(b) Decide on priority teaching area(s)

This is perhaps the most controversial part of the procedure. Which aspect should James's teacher start with? Should she concentrate on building up a bank of sight words, on letter sounds and phonics or on approaches based on reading with and for the child? Ideally the answer should be all three so that tuition moves on a broad front and takes account of the interaction between linguistic, visual and phonic information. For example, the ideal plan for James at this stage would consist of the following three main elements:

- Assisted reading of many easy books as described in Chapter Eleven.
- Repetitive reading and writing practice of a limited number of sight words until they have really been mastered.
- Equally systematic and repetitive practice of initial letter sounds through 'I Spy' games and the illustrated alphabet described in Chapter Seven.

With so little time for individual instruction, teachers may have to decide which of the elements should receive the highest priority. James's teacher chose to start with the introduction of a limited number of sight words and, once this aspect was established, to move on to systematic practice of letter sounds in conjunction with continued reading of stories which contained the words James had learnt. His teacher's task was made much easier because James's parents were keen to help and were able to read to James and, later, to read with him.

The class teacher in charge of some 30 children has usually only time to make a 'five minute' plan for the pupil with reading difficulties. It therefore becomes particularly important to decide on the highest priority for that pupil and to stick to the priority teaching area for long enough to enable the child with learning difficulties to make progress. When a pupil struggles with reading, it is tempting to switch from one task to the next in the hope that something else will work better. This can result in an approach described as 'a little of a lot' where the pupil is not given enough time to learn any one task. Children with learning difficulties need more time to practise the same objective until it is really learnt and, provided that the initial assessment of the pupil's level of reading is accurate, these children will progress when they have the chance to practise a specified task for a sufficiently long period of time; in other words, when they have an opportunity to learn 'a lot of a little'.

But this approach does have pitfalls. When the learning task has been narrowed down to only one specific area, the danger is that the overall picture of the nature of reading is forgotten. If, for example, the teacher concentrates on a limited set of words then it is tempting to keep on adding to the list of sight words and to forget to ensure that other aspects in turn receive intensive emphasis. Similarly, if letter sounds and phonics are taken as the priority area, it will be important to arrange practice in such a way that the words exemplifying phonic regularities become part of the pupil's automatic sight vocabulary. And all along the teacher should not forget that the main purpose of teaching is to help the pupil understand the meaning of the text. The sight words and phonics must, therefore, be encountered in the context of 'real' reading of stories and other information. It can be seen that getting the balance right is not easy. Although the teacher is guided by the assessment of the pupil's level of reading and particular strengths and weaknesses with regard to reading strategies, in the end the teacher has to make the decision about priorities and the ways of ensuring that all aspects of reading are included.

(c) Plan learning steps

Having decided which aspect is to receive concentrated practice, the teacher will next consider ways of subdividing the task into sufficiently small learning steps. In the case study of James, his teacher chose the words to be included in the initial set of 12 words and the order of introducing them. These decisions were based on the teacher's judgement and knowledge of James. His teacher could have chosen a different set of words or a smaller or larger number of words. Therefore, initial decisions remain to some extent arbitrary and only records of progress will indicate whether the teacher was right. If the child is not progressing, the clearly specified learning target forms a starting point for subdividing the task into still smaller steps or for considering alternative methods or priorities.

If the teacher has chosen a sufficiently small number of relevant words, the planning of learning steps, as described in the case study of James, is relatively straightforward for new sight vocabulary. Additionally, however, later chapters about the teaching of phonics, spelling and handwriting also follow similar procedures and the manual outlines some suggested learning sequences for these aspects.

When planning a programme, it is useful to think of the learning of skills in terms of a five stage hierarchy as described by Haring *et al,* (1978). The learning hierarchy is presented in Table 6.4.

Table 6.4:
Learning a new skill (from Haring *et al*, 1978)

Acquisition:	The pupil begins to learn the skill and is starting to perform accurately.
Fluency:	The pupil performs the skill accurately and fluently.
Maintenance:	The pupil continues to perform fluently over a long period of time without any teacher assistance.
Generalization:	The pupil can apply the new skill to different tasks following instruction.
Adaptation:	The pupil applies the skill in new settings without any instruction.

In the case study of James, the learning steps were arranged in a cumulative way so that words learned earlier were incorporated in later sentence building with a further set of new words. This ensured that the requirements of the first three headings in Table 6.4 were met, i.e., a set of sight words received massed practice until they were read fluently and without hesitation and then the same words were deliberately included in further activities to maintain the skill. Of course, another important reason for including the 'old' words in further practice was to make the sentence building activities more interesting and linguistically relevant.

The last two headings in Table 6.4, *generalization* and *adaptation*, remind us of the limitations of instruction which is not transferred to a variety of situations. Until James reads the words he has learnt in a selection of books, with and without direct help from teachers and parents, we cannot be sure that he has really mastered what we have taught him. This is why it is essential to complement the practice of a specified task with assisted reading of as many books as possible. The teacher can then ensure that the pupil uses newly learnt skills in many contexts, for example, by keeping at hand the record book which lists the sight vocabulary mastered and, if necessary, helping the pupil to refer to it as to a dictionary when the words are encountered in a new story.

(d) Choose teaching methods and teach

James's teacher introduced a rich variety of methods for teaching the 12 specified sight words. In this way James was not bored by the limited task and his motivation was enhanced both by his success and by the part he played in helping his teacher to record the progress. All the teaching methods were planned in such a way that James could complete his assignments successfully. For example, his teacher made sure that James attained reasonably high 'scores' when words were checked over and, if he could not read a word or if he made a mistake, his teacher would help him to read the word using prompts which avoided comments such as 'no, that's wrong!'.

The choice of methods depends on teacher preference and the circumstances of teaching such as the amount of time available for instruction and the extent to which practice can take place within the ordinary classroom as part of other class or group activities. If parents or other helpers are involved, it is possible to introduce a wider range of methods. There are no hard and fast rules about methods of teaching as long as the pupil feels successful and as long as there is progress. While the selection of methods in this manual should provide a good starting point for the teacher, there are many other possible ways of enhancing repetition which have not been included here.

(e) Record and evaluate progress

It can be difficult to determine the criterion, or standard, of success required to show that the pupil has really learnt the task and, again, the decision has to be left to teacher judgement and knowledge of the individual pupil. How many times will the pupil have to give the correct response and how quick and fluent should the response be before it is felt that a particular objective has been learnt? James's teacher chose as her criterion ten 'ticks' for each sight word but she could have chosen a different criterion or she could have changed it in the light of her observations when teaching James. If the standard set by the teacher is too high then time can be wasted in unnecessary repetition and, if it is too low, then the pupil will not have had the opportunity to really master the task. The difficulty of deciding about these matters can, however, be alleviated by a record-keeping system which checks at a later date whether the learnt task has still been retained. This form of record keeping involves a more long-term plan for each objective. Three items are required:

(a) The *date* work on a particular target task was commenced.

(b) The *date* the task was mastered, i.e. the criterion of success was achieved. This may be the same day, a few days later or a week later, but too long spent on one objective usually indicates that it is too difficult and that a modification is necessary.

(c) The *date* a check was made that the task was still mastered. This may be a few days later, one week later or a month later. The time interval is not crucial as long as a system of checking that the skill or knowledge has been retained is built into the record-keeping system. If not retained, relearning becomes necessary but this is usually done in a much shorter time than the original learning.

It is tempting merely to tick objectives as they are mastered; this takes up just as much time but conveys far less information than a date. For example, the time lapsed between commencing the learning of a task and its mastery gives the teacher an indication of the rate at which the pupil is learning and shows whether the pupil can cope with larger or smaller learning steps. It is also useful to provide a space in the record-keeping system for notes on methods used, including any changes in method or materials. In Table 6.5 below we have again used the case study of James to illustrate one format of this type of record keeping.

Table 6.5:
James's reading record

| LEARNING TARGETS | STANDARD | COMMENTS | RECORD WITH DATES: | | |
			WORKING ON	MASTERED	CHECKED
I am going to school	Ten 'ticks' for each word				
the bus stop is	as above				
teacher big at etc. etc. further targets	as above				

It is now possible to evaluate whether the pupil is making progress with the specified task. If progress is good, the teacher will move to the next objective in the programme. If the target is still not being attained, a re-examination of the diagram in Table 6.2 will indicate what action can be taken. The arrows in the diagram point to the aspects which may need reconsideration:

(a) Reassess the child to make sure you have identified the correct level of reading.
(b) Consider whether there are more appropriate priority teaching areas.
(c) Think of more interesting learning materials or smaller learning steps.
(d) Reconsider teaching methods and ways of enhancing interest.

Conclusion

This chapter has made use of a detailed case study as a basis for outlining the planning and recording involved in step-by-step approaches to learning difficulties. Later chapters in the manual will follow the theme by providing further examples of teaching sequences and methods of record keeping. We have emphasized the limitations of this approach, in particular, the pitfalls of losing sight of the nature of reading so that the programme becomes limited to only one narrow aspect. It must also be pointed out that we have given the reader only a taste of what is commonly called curriculum-based approaches to learning difficulties. Because more detail is beyond the scope of this manual, references for further reading are provided in the Bibliography section (Ainscow and Tweddle, 1984; Haring *et al*, 1980).

Chapter 7

The use of phonics at Stage I and Stage II

Introduction

The teaching of phonics in reading draws attention to regular correspondence between spoken sounds and their written representations. The term 'phonics' is here used as the global heading for all aspects of sound/symbol correspondence, from initial discrimination of letter sounds to sequential blending of polysyllabic words.

Many children need little direct phonic teaching. They work out the rules pragmatically for themselves. The analytical method of teaching phonics helps the child to do so and starts from the child's knowledge of whole words. The sound represented by a given written symbol is deduced from examining the appearance of the whole word, listening to the sound of it, and pronouncing it carefully (e.g. 'boat'). Analogies can then be made with familiar words with the same spelling pattern (e.g. 'coat'). All the more complex rules of pronouncing written English are normally learned in this way.

Children who experience difficulty in learning to read may not be able to take advantage of incidental learning following the analytical method of teaching. Their memory for linking visual and auditory symbols may not be sufficient to retain a given written symbol and the sound it represents in the context of the whole word. As a consequence, on seeing unfamiliar words with the same spelling pattern, they cannot use the analogy because they are not able to remember what sound the spelling pattern represents. These children need a more direct and repetitive method of teaching phonics.

Synthetic phonic methods start from single letters and digraphs (e.g. sh, th, ee). The sounds most commonly used with the written forms are learned and words are built up or synthesized from the elements (e.g. ba – t, sp – oo – n, ch – ur – ch, scr – a – p, ex – ten – sion). Rules are taught, not deduced. Phonic reading schemes usually advocate this method.

As illustrated in Table 4.1 on page 14, the use of phonics is but one aspect of the process of learning to read. The pupil is often able to read fluently by using language and general knowledge cues so that she predicts accurately new words from context and initial letter cues (e.g. 'It was so hot in bed that John could not sl...' 'We had fish and ch... for dinner'.) At the beginning stages this should be encouraged. If the child does not naturally use contextual cues, we can help by re-reading the sentence for her and stopping at the unknown word which she has to guess from initial letters and word shape (For example 'It was so hot in bed that John could not sl... What do you think it could be?')

It is not necessary to teach every possible letter combination. Pupils with reading difficulties may initially need very careful teaching of phonics using the synthetic method which includes individual letters, consonant blends and digraphs and the most commonly used vowel digraphs (see Jackson's Phonic Skills mentioned earlier on page 11 for illustrations of these terms). After that, pupils can often work out further 'rules' for themselves in the context of extensive reading practice. In other words, they are now ready for the more natural analytical forms of learning.

If a pupil needs to be taught phonics in a detailed and repetitive manner, it is particularly important to ensure that any possible hearing loss has been identified. It is not uncommon for children to have a fluctuating hearing loss associated with catarrhal blockage or, in a few cases, an unidentified sensory – neural hearing loss may account for the child's inability to discriminate between letter sounds which are within a certain frequency range. If you have any doubts about the child's ability to hear well, arrange for her to see the school's Clinical Medical Officer or ask the parents to take the child to their family doctor.

We shall follow the framework of reading stages outlined in Chapter Four (Finding the right level) and summarized in Table 4.1 on page 14 when considering the teaching of phonics. This chapter describes methods for the Stage I and Stage II reader and the next chapter will provide suggestions for Stages III and IV.

Stage I: Pre-reading

1. *Auditory recognition of initial letter sounds: 'I Spy'*

If the pupil did not pass the 'I Spy' test described in Chapter Four, page 16, he will need extra help in learning to 'hear' the first sound of the spoken word. The following games, suggested by Muriel Bridge, are designed to help develop this ability. They may be played with the individual child or a small group of two or three pupils. Only initial letter sounds are used, not the alphabetical names of the letters.

Easy Kim's Game

A tray of four objects is assembled, each of which begins with the same sound, e.g. saucer, sock, spoon, salt. The child is asked to name each object. The teacher repeats each name (correcting if necessary), but slightly emphasizing the first sound by sustaining it: 'sssaucer', 'sssock', etc. The child repeats this. When all the objects have been named in this way, he is asked which sound they all start with. The teacher may need to rephrase the question several times and repeat the naming of the objects, overemphasizing the initial sound even more. In a few cases the teacher may have to tell the child what the initial sound is. When this happens, the procedure will have to be repeated, possibly on several further occasions. The tray of objects is called the 'sssss tray'.

The teacher has some reserve objects which may or may not begin with s. The child examines and names each object and is helped to exaggerate the first sound to determine whether it belong to the 'sssss tray' or not. Other s items could include: sweets, scissors, stone, seeds. It is important to select the non – s items carefully. Avoid similar sounds, such as sh, and choose a strong contrast, such as m. Sustainable sounds are easier to 'hear': a,e,f,h,i,l,m,n,o,r,s,v.

For the purpose of the usual Kim's Game, the 'ssss tray' is covered over and the child tries to recall all the objects on the tray.

Easy Clue Game

Once the child can 'hear' the initial s sound in the way suggested above, he can play the Clue Game. The teacher says: 'It begins with 'sssss' and it is ...' (e.g. a boy's name, a girl's name, an animal, in the sky, where you wash up in the kitchen).

The easy Kim's Game and the easy Clue Games can be repeated for different initial letter sounds. There is no need to do this for all the letters of the alphabet. Once it is felt that the child completes the task with ease, he is ready for the next games.

The Home Game

The following games involve discrimination between two or more sounds.

– The pupil allocates each object from a jumbled assortment to its proper HOME: the 'ssss tray' or the 'mmmm tray', etc. He is encouraged to name each object, exaggerating the first sound to decide which is the correct HOME.

– The teacher prepares two trays of objects chosen by initial sound but *two* objects are in the wrong HOME. The pupil must find which objects are in the wrong HOME and return them to the correct one.

The game is extended by introducing a third or fourth tray.

Guess Which One

Once four different sounds have been isolated in this way, the teacher presents a group of four objects, one for each sound. The pupil is asked to pick up or point at the object for which the teacher has given the first sound.

Hard Kim's Game

Cover the tray of four objects (each beginning with a different sound). The teacher asks: 'Can you remember what was on the tray beginning with ...?' The difficulty of this task can be increased by adding more objects to the tray.

Another version of this game is for the teacher to ask: 'Is there something on the tray beginning with ...?' Make sure the answer is not always 'yes'.

Picture games

As soon as the pupil can isolate first sounds using concrete objects, the range of games can be extended by using *pictures* collected by the child or the teacher. Commercially produced pictures can be obtained from many educational publishers.

When the child is able to play the normal game of 'I Spy', you can test her using the task described on page 16. If the test is passed the child is ready to learn the written representations of the letter sounds.

2. Auditory sound blending

The child is required to merge the separate sounds that make up a word in order to say the complete word. The words are not presented in a written form to the child; the teacher says the sounds pausing between each sound segment and the child then says the whole word.

If the child did not pass the test of auditory sound blending on page 16, more practice will be needed in this area. The task may have been unfamiliar to the child and you may find that, after some further instruction, she understands the task requirements and is then able to blend the segments of the words quite well.

Sometimes children can have difficulty with sound discrimination and blending because their attention control is poor. In other words, they have not learnt to listen carefully. To help the child, ask her to sit opposite you and to look carefully at your mouth as you say the segments of the word. (Note the importance of making sure that the child's hearing has been previously tested.)

When teaching the child to blend the segments of the word, it is better to start with longer words which are divided into big 'chunks' than short words where the segments consist of individual letter sounds. For example, the child is likely to find lemon – ade easier than st – op. We have listed some of common longer words in Table 7.1 which you can use as a start for teaching sound blending.

Table 7.1:
Sound blending

aero – plane	chim – pan – zee
break – fast	hand – ker – chief
bed – room	beau – ti – ful
after – noon	im – por – tant
play – ground	mo – tor – bike
lemon – ade	hos – pit – al
adven – ture	pho – to – graph
car – pet	un – der – stand
seven – teen	te – le – phone
cheer – ful	mar – ma – lade
cur – tain	yes – ter – day

If the child continues to have difficulty with sound blending, you will have to shorten the one second pause between the segments of the word so that the segments nearly merge together as you say them. Always help the child to complete the word successfully even if you are virtually saying the word for her first. When the child is able to merge the word segments, you can gradually lengthen your pauses again until the child can blend the segments into one word when you pause for about one second between them.

It is not necessary to labour with the sound blending task for too long. If the child continues to have difficulty when you repeat the test on page 16 after some teaching, note this in your records and move on to the next stage of phonics. The child is likely to have later difficulty when required to blend sounds represented by written symbols. At that stage you can choose to return to this task and you will know that the child is likely to require a highly repetitive approach where the blending of a small number of words is practised as part of a drill procedure.

3. Rhymes and non-rhymes

The child should listen carefully to the teacher and repeat distinctly the pairs of words mentioned on page 16 in order to discriminate between rhymes and non-rhymes. Children who are unable to perform this task are likely to have difficulty in developing phonic or spelling skills. The following activities are suggested:

Silly nursery rhymes

Choose a familiar rhyme written in rhyming couplets. Alter the second rhyme to another non-rhyming word. The child should correct you triumphantly! For example:

> 'Little Miss Muffet
> sat on a chair'

Avoid non-rhyming verses like Old Macdonald. Other suitable verses are Ding Dong Bell, Jack and Jill, Mary Mary, Humpty Dumpty, Diddle Diddle Dumpling. This is a good game for children and parents to enjoy at home. It assumes, however, that children have had much previous opportunity to learn nursery rhymes.

Picture pairs

Present *pictures* of pairs of objects. The child names the pictures and collects pairs that rhyme. Before beginning, check on names and pronunciation, especially if the child speaks with a regional dialect or has difficulties with speech articulation. For example:

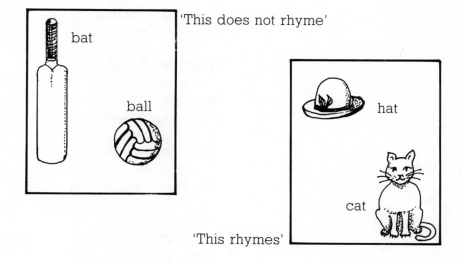

'This does not rhyme'

bat

ball

hat

cat

'This rhymes'

Find the rhymes

Present sets of *pictures* in arrays of three or four, each with one non-rhyming 'odd-man-out', which the child must identify. For example:

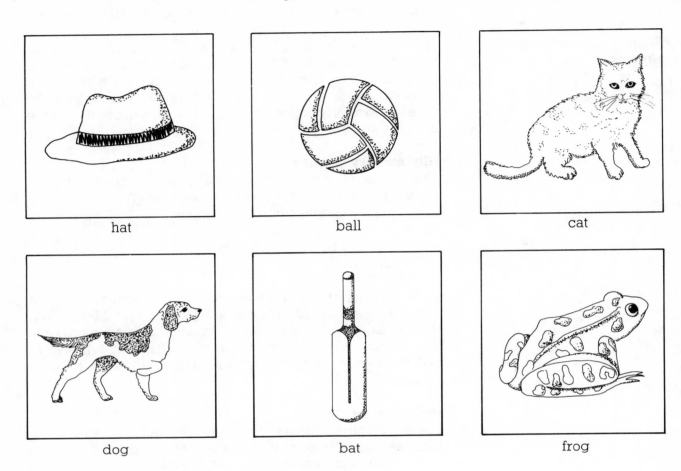

hat	ball	cat
dog	bat	frog

Rhyming Snap

Pictures similar to those used in rhyming pairs are drawn singly on blank playing cards. Games of Snap or Pelmanism can then be played.

Rhyming riddles

An oral game which may be played with a group of children at school or by parents and child at home. The child supplies the final rhyming word in each couplet. For example:

Sammy Cox put on his *...socks.*
Mrs Mill paid the *...bill.*
Little Ben writes with a *...pen.*
Uncle Paul is very *...tall.*
In my house there is a *...mouse.*

Note that all these rhyming games are purely oral and *no* reading is involved. There is therefore no need to confine words to easy phonic patterns.

Stage II: The beginning reader
1. Single letter sounds

Having learnt to 'hear' the first sound of a word in the 'I Spy' game, the child is ready to move on to recognizing the written representation of the letter sound. If the child already knows many of the written letter sounds, the criterion referenced test on page 18 will help you identify which letters have not been learnt.

Where to start
Select no more than three unknown letters of distinctive and contrasting shape and sound (e.g. s,m,a). The beginning reader will find it easier to learn sustainable sounds (e.g. m,f,s,n) rather than sounds which can be pronounced only briefly (e.g. b,c,t).

The illustrated alphabet
The child gradually builds up his own individual pack of letter cards, starting with the first three unknown letters. Each card in the pack has on one side the letter and a picture of an object which begins with that letter. On the reverse side of the card, only the letter is shown. This is illustrated below:

Picture side   Reverse side

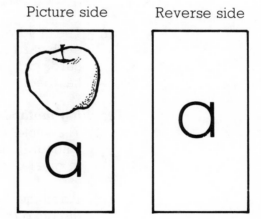

Children often like to select their own 'clue' object for a given letter and to draw the object for themselves on the picture side of the card. Those who are not good at drawing may prefer to make the choice of object and to have the teacher draw it. There are commercially produced pictures which can be used for this purpose. We have included at the end of this chapter a set of alphabet cards produced by the Leicestershire Literacy Support Service. These cards can be reproduced so that the child has his own individual set.

Teaching methods: picture side up
  (a) Select the first three letter cards to be learnt (e.g. m,s,a).

  (b) Place the cards picture side *up* on the table.

  (c) Point at the <u>a</u> card and say 'a – apple';the child repeats 'a – apple'.
       Point at the <u>s</u> card and say 's – snake';the child repeats 's – snake'.

Point at the <u>m</u> card and say 'm – milk';the child repeats 'm – milk'.

(d)   Sustain the sound (e.g. mmm) and ask the child to point at the right card. Repeat this for the other two cards. Continue in random order for all three cards until the child always points to the right card easily and quickly.

(e)   Now point to each letter card and ask the child to make the correct sound. Repeat until the child's responses are fluent.

(f)   Follow the same procedure with three more cards.

(g)   You now have a pack of six cards. Select any three cards at random and check whether the child can still recall the sounds with ease (with the picture side up so that the mnemonic clue is easily available).

(h)   Continue to add cards to the pack in this way (only using the picture side of the cards) and repeat the activity daily for a few minutes over a period of a week or more.

(i)   The child will learn to respond with increasing speed to each card until you are able to flick through the pack of cards and the child's response to the letter/picture clue has become instant.

Teaching methods: the 'quick flip'

(a)   The child is now ready to learn to recognize letters without their picture clues. Start again with the three original cards.

(b)   Place the cards picture side *down* on the table so that the child can only see the letter on the reverse side of the card.

(c)   Ask the child to say the correct sound for each letter. If he cannot recall the sound, allow him to make a 'quick flip', i.e. take a very quick look at the picture side of the card. Having seen the picture clue, the child is able to give the correct sound. Continue to rehearse this until the three cards require no more 'quick flips'. The child may need several days of practice before he can automatically give the right sound without reference to the picture clue.

(d)   Gradually add more cards to the pack, always continuing to revise previously learnt cards.

(e)   The child will often develop 'x-ray eyes' visualizing the clue picture on the other side of the card and so remembering it by heart. As he becomes more proficient, you can gradually increase the speed of the child's response to each card. Eventually he will be able to flick through the whole pack of cards saying each letter sound instantly.

Note that teachers may prefer to introduce the 'quick flip' much earlier in the procedure, for example, after the first three letters with picture clues have been learnt. The teaching method then consists of alternating between learning initial letters with picture clues and practising automatic recognition of single letters without picture clues.

Extra games for reinforcement

(a) Another version of 'I Spy': The teacher says, 'I Spy ...something beginning with ...' but instead of saying the letter sound, she shows a letter card or writes the letter.

(b) Games such as Pairs, Snap or Happy Families can be played by making further sets of letter cards. It is essential that pupils always say the letter *sound* aloud when pairing up the cards so that they do not succeed with the task on the basis of visual matching alone. (*Games for Developing Reading Skills*, published by NARE, provide detailed descriptions of these types of activities. The publisher's address can be found under the Resources heading.)

Dictation

The child should be able to read and write the letter sounds before we can be sure that they have really been learnt. Written practice can be started as soon as the first letters of the illustrated alphabet have been introduced. It is at times recommended that the older pupil who has reading problems at this level should learn simultaneously to read and write a particular letter sound. The task can be too demanding for the younger child and the teacher may decide to introduce the written work at a later stage, for example, when the child has learnt to recognize most letter sounds. Once the child can form the letters correctly, we want her to be able to write them from memory. We can dictate the letter sounds in random order or dictate a list of interesting words for which the child writes the first letter only. The task of learning to write letter sounds from dictation can also be divided into small learning steps.

Transfer of learning to the reading book

The transfer of letter recognition from the set of cards to the reading book does not always happen automatically. *As soon as* the child has learnt a few letter sounds, the teacher can scan ahead to locate a word beginning with one of the newly learnt letters. The word should occur towards the end of a phrase or sentence so that there are enough meaningful cues based on context. The teacher covers up the word except for the first letter. The pupil is encouraged to 'guess' from preceding meaning and the initial letter. Records of the child's progress will indicate which letter sounds can be treated in this way. With practice over a period of time, the child should acquire the habit of speedy integration of cues based on context and initial letters.

2. Introducing word building

Before starting work at this stage, ensure that the pupil can play 'I Spy', can identify single letter sounds and use those sounds as initial letter cues in reading practice. When introducing word building skills, we should continue to encourage the use of context and initial impressions of words so that the pupil does not learn to rely on 'sounding out' the entire word as her only strategy.

Materials: You will need commercially produced plastic cut-out letters or letters written individually on fairly small cards (e.g. 2cm×2cm).

Learning sequence: (We are grateful to Margaret Naylor for these suggestions.)

(a)   Talk about the short vowel sounds (a̲,e̲,i̲,o̲,u̲) and explain their importance. The child can look through his reading book to check that every word contains at least one vowel. (Note that in some words like 'my' the y̲ is considered a vowel).

(b)   Select vowel a̲ along with the consonants t̲,m̲,p̲,c̲,b̲,f̲,s̲,r̲,g̲. Place the consonant cards (or plastic letters) on the table underneath each other. Move the a̲ card to the side of each consonant in turn and blend together the consonant and the vowel. For example:

```
p - a   -   pa
c - a   -   ca
m - a   -   ma
```

Continue to blend until the child can say without any hesitation or pause between the two sounds: *pa, ca, ma, fa, sa,* etc. It may take several sessions for the child's response to become so easy and automatic that there is no need for prior demonstration. It is particularly important that she learns to merge the initial consonant with the vowel; this avoids distortion (e.g. me – ah) and the pitfall of teaching the child to sound out words letter by letter (e.g. w – h – i – s – k – e – r instead of whi – sk – er).

(c)   Introduce final consonants t̲,n̲,g̲,p̲,d̲.

```
Blend   pa - t   -   pat
        ca - n   -   can
        ma - p   -   map   etc.
```

This step should follow easily from the previous one. Repeat in random order until the child's responses are fluent. It can take several sessions.

(d)   Let the child make her own words by arranging the letters thus:

```
p
c           t
m     a     n
s           g
f
```

Take one letter from the left column to blend with a̲. Add the third letter from the final column. Make sure that the initial consonant and the vowel are always pronounced as one unit.

(e) Step (d) can be consolidated with work cards if required. The child writes her own words and later reads them out to the teacher.

(f) Continue steps (b) to (e) with each vowel in turn.

(g) Once all the above steps have been mastered, introduce the 'sound dictionary'. Draw five columns on a sheet of paper headed by each of the vowels: a̠,e̠,i̠,o̠,u̠. Dictate three letter words with the short vowel, e.g. 'map', 'let', 'cup', 'hot', 'six'. (Lists of words can be obtained from phonic resource books mentioned in the Bibliography. It is however preferable to dictate words taken from the child's reading book, for example, the 'Gay Way' and 'Reading 360' readers contain a large number of appropriate words.) The child repeats the dictated word aloud and listens carefully. She then identifies the vowel in each word, finds the appropriate column on the 'sound dictionary' sheet and writes the word. A few children may confuse similar sounds such as e̠ and i̠ or o̠ and u̠. Encourage the child to look closely at you as you pronounce the word and to attend to the 'feel' of the word in his mouth as he repeats it. If the confusion persists, note this in your records and move on to the next stage. When reading a meaningful text the child should be able to compensate for this weakness by visual memory and/or contextual cues.

(h) The child is now ready to write simple sentences from dictation. For example:

> 'The cat and the dog sat on the mat'
> 'He had a pan with a lid'
> 'It is fun to sit in the sun'

Whenever possible, use words from the child's reading books as this will help her transfer what she has learnt to more independent reading practice. When the child can read and spell the short sentences, she will have acquired the concept of written language as a sequence of letter sounds which merge to make distinct and meaningful words.

(i) The use of the 'sound dictionary' and dictation can now be extended to phonics at Stage III level if required. By introducing initial and final consonant blends and digraphs, we can build up an extensive reading vocabulary based on the short medial vowel (e.g. 'shop', 'trick', 'lamp', 'brush', 'spend' – see the next chapter).

3. Using known sight words as a basis for word building

A few children may remain unable to blend single sounds into short words despite carefully structured teaching. Such children might respond to the approach tried by Glyn's teacher.

Glyn had a sight vocabulary which included the phonically regular words 'red', 'pig', 'cat', 'hen'. Although he could read these words, he could not read new words consisting of the same consonant – vowel – consonant structures. He could identify most single letters by their sound and was just becoming adept at 'I Spy'. His teacher used 'cat' as a starting point in the following way:

(a) Can you tell me this word? (cat)
(b) Listen to the sounds in 'cat' – c – a – t
(c) Now you say it
(d) Let's say it like this: c – a – t – c – ca – cat
(e) Say it after me
(f) Point to the letters in 'cat' as I say them
(g) You say the letters and see if I can point to them
(h) Now guess which word on the page I am saying: h – e – n
(g) Use each of the known sight words in this way.

By alternating between well-known sight words and their constituent sounds, the teacher enabled Glyn to grasp the concept of phonic blending. This method can also be useful for children who have difficulty in distinguishing between short vowel sounds. Sight words containing the target vowel become key words for reading or writing new short vowel words. Any reading scheme which contains a reasonable number of consonant – vowel – consonant words is suitable for this purpose, for example 'One, Two, Three and Away'; 'Gay Way'; 'Link Up'; 'Reading 360'.

Record keeping

Each of the teaching sequences in this chapter can be recorded in the way described in Chapter Six, i.e. by defining steps in the form of learning targets, by setting a standard of performance to indicate when the target has been mastered, and by recording progress with dates under the headings of *Working on, Mastered, Checked*. This format is illustrated in Table 7.2 with reference to the sequence for introducing word building on page 55. To allow more spaces for recording, it is better to turn the paper so that the longest side is in a horizontal position. It is by no means suggested that teachers should follow the exact format of our illustration and many will devise their own systems based on other symbols or codes such as using different coloured pens to mark progress. It is the way of thinking about record keeping which is important and not the exact format that the record sheet takes.

Table 7.2:
A record of consonant—vowel—consonant word building

LEARNING TARGETS	STANDARD	COMMENTS	WORKING ON	MASTERED	CHECKED
pat, can, map, man, sat, pan, cat, fan, fat	Reads fluently at least 3 times, in any order				
pen, net, red, leg, pet, hen, set, men, let	As above				
pot, dog, top, fog, hot, got, job, not, hop	As above				
pig, tin, big, fit, bin, sit, win, bit, bin	As above				
bus, cup, run, sun, cut, hug, bun, but, hut	As above				
The 'sound dictionary': see page 57.	At least 5 words for each vowel located correctly.				
Words from the above targets read in any order.	All words correct and fluent (but in some cases allowing some errors - see page 57.)				
The pupil can write simple sentences from dictation, e.g. 'It is fun to sit in the sun'.	Usually all correct.				
At Stage III further targets can be introduced for initial and final consonant blends and digraphs — see page 68.					

ILLUSTRATED LETTER CARDS

It is assumed that the child can 'hear' the first sounds of words, as when playing 'I Spy'.

Each child has his or her own set of letter cards.

Each letter sound is learnt as the initial sound of a picture whose shape closely resembles the letter shape.

The letter may be coloured boldly, but the picture should be left as a black-and-white 'background' prompt.

(The letter cards and instructions were designed by Angela R. White.)

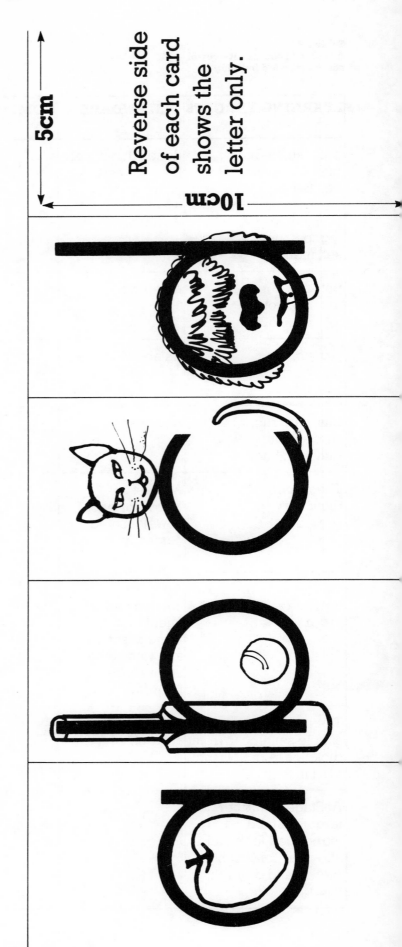

Reverse side of each card shows the letter only.

5cm

10cm

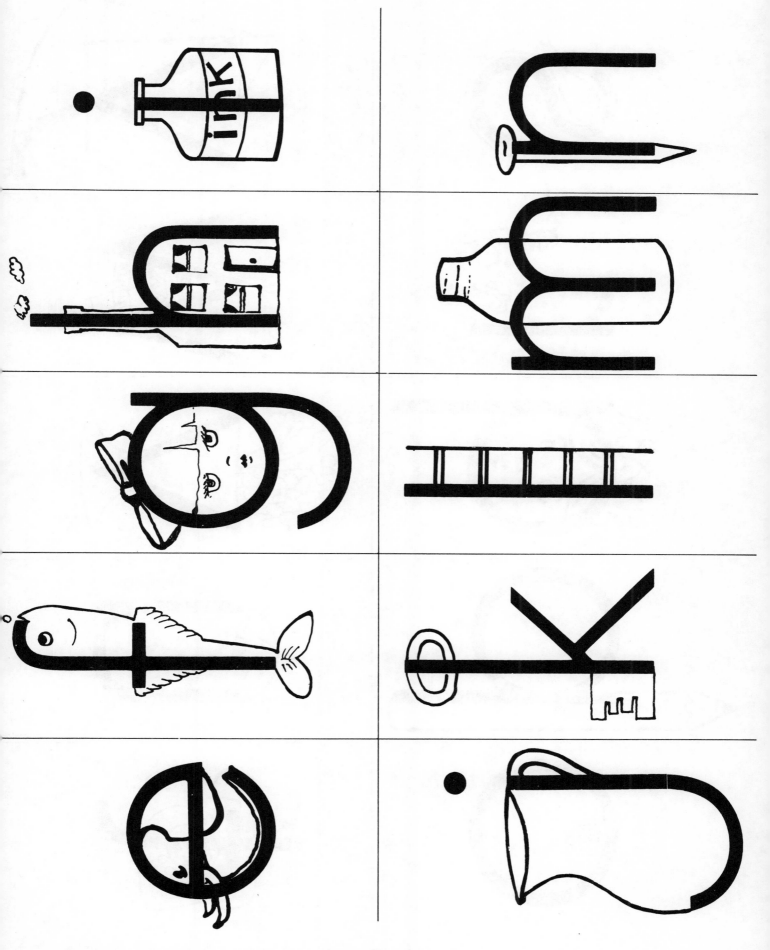

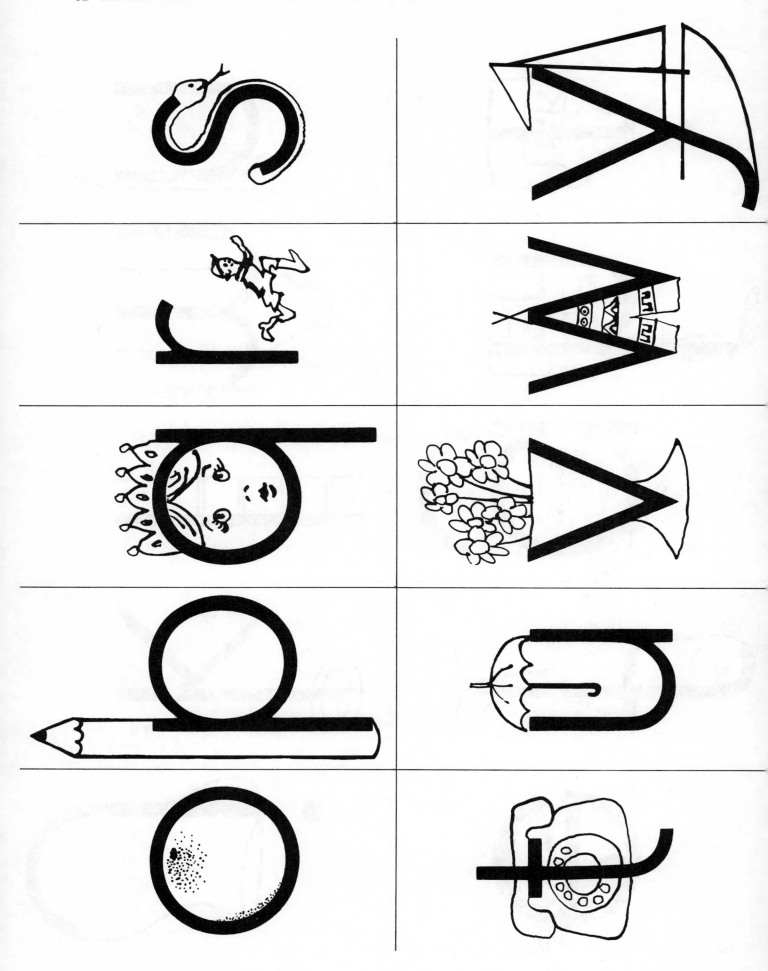

Chapter 8   Phonics at Stage III and Stage IV

Introduction

As pupils reach Stages III and IV they are beginning to integrate reading into automatic processes consisting of previously learned skills and knowledge. Fluent readers absorb and apply phonics without necessarily being able to state them. They may learn, for example, that ch is pronounced k in 'chemist' because they have previously met the same combination in 'Christmas' and so no overt rules about these kinds of regularities need to be explained or memorized. Our task at this stage is, therefore, to identify only those children who are not picking up phonic regularities so easily. As described below, we can determine the children's needs for more specific phonic practice by listening to them read and examining their particular approaches to reading.

Stage III: The intermediate reader

CONCEPTS AND APPROACHES	VISUAL WORD RECOGNITION	PHONICS
Infers from context and meaning and uses phonics when necessary.	Extensive sight vocabulary from the middle sections of reading schemes.	Reads and spells: – consonant blends – consonant digraphs – vowel digraphs – silent 'e'

The extract above from Table 4.1 summarizes the skills which pupils will have acquired by the time they reach the *end* of Stage III. It is included as a reminder that language cues, automatic visual memory and phonics are considered interdependent in the process of learning to read. If the individual pupil experiences difficulties in one area, other areas may compensate for the weakness. For example, phonic analysis and contextual cues may help the pupil who struggles with the automatic visual aspects of word recognition.

It is assumed that children who are making steady progress will have reached a similar level in all three columns. Children whose phonic skills are weak, however, may have come to rely excessively on contextual guessing or on waiting for the teacher to supply the words they cannot read. Conversely those with good phonic skills sometimes continue to analyse and build up words which should have become part of their automatic sight vocabulary and so their reading style remains slow and laborious. As much of written English does not fit the phonic 'rules', it is important at this stage of learning to encourage flexible guesswork. In addition, immediate visual recognition of words should receive continued practice through the kinds of activities described in Chapter Five. In this way all areas of reading are developed in parallel.

The learning of phonics also links with the learning of spelling described in Chapter Nine. Poor spellers who have found the early stages of phonics difficult are likely to have a continued need to study words in phonic family groups, and, as described in the previous chapter, if pupils have marked difficulty with remembering phonic regularities, written practice and dictation form an important part of instruction.

1. Deciding what to teach

Pupils at the beginning of Stage III are well on their way to learning basic reading skills. Up to now they may have needed deliberate and detailed help with sight words, single letter sounds and word building. Now they are likely to be able to benefit from incidental learning through plenty of reading practice and they may already be using many of the Stage III phonic structures. Therefore the teacher's first task is to assess which letter combinations the pupil still needs to learn. This can be done in two ways. The first and preferred method involves listening to the pupil read and noting down errors and approaches. The advantage of this method is that it shows whether errors are phonically based or whether they are caused by other factors. Checklists are the second way of identifying those letter combinations which still need to be learnt. Although this may seem an easier method, some specialist teachers now consider it to be too divorced from the 'real' reading process. Both methods are described and illustrated below.

Classifying errors when hearing the child read

The fluent Stage III or IV reader expects reading to make sense and uses context as an aid to identify unfamiliar words. Phonics in turn are used to check contextual cue guesses by looking at word structure in terms of elements of meaning (e.g. horse – shoe not horses – hoe); syllables (e.g. pho – to – graph) and letter-strings (e.g. str – eng – th). By noting down pupil errors when hearing the child read, we can determine to what extent he or she has reached this standard and which aspects still need careful teaching.

For the purpose of examining errors a slightly more difficult text can be chosen. Ideally the child's reading should be tape recorded for later analysis and errors marked on a copy of the text. The following are some usual ways of marking errors:

> horse
> house (substitution)
> (house) (circle non-response)
> h – ou – s (phonic strategy noted)
> tick for self-corrections

Consider these two questions:

– Does the reader expect to make sense of the text?
– What does the reader do when confronted by an unknown word?

Some examples taken from longer text analyses

The following examples are extracts from much longer error analyses made by teachers. They have been chosen to illustrate the process of planning remediation from observation of errors. The remediation takes the form of individual work for the pupil, practice to be done with parents at home or teaching points to be made when the child reads to the teacher.

> Debbie: 'What happy noo?'
> Text: What happens now?

Teacher's notes: Debbie does not seem to expect meaning. She substitutes with a real word which has the same initial letter (happy/happens). The second substitution also has the correct initial letter but it is a nonsense word (noo/now). *Phonics:* Debbie seems to know and use initial letter sounds. Is she confusing ow and oo? *Action:* Debbie needs to talk about the story and predict the content before reading it. When reading together, Debbie's teacher or parent can scan ahead and help her guess appropriate words, e.g. 'the girl went out to pl..'. Phonics such as initial consonant blends can be introduced in the context of words which appear in her reading book.

> Robin: 'We have e – n – o – u – g – h enough m – o – n – e – y
>   money to get s – w – e – e – t – s sweets'
>   (letter – by – letter sounding).'
> Text: We haven't enough money to buy sweets.

Teacher's notes: Robin has developed a habit of sounding each letter before he makes a guess. The sounding out is inefficient and hinders reading fluency. Yet, remarkably, he reads the words correctly. Robin seems unwilling to take a risk with guessing whole words. His caution may be justified in view of the reading of 'haven't' as 'have' and 'buy' as 'get'. *Action:* Encourage contextual guessing. Repeated reading of an easier text should improve fluency. Teach phonically regular words such as those presented in Table 8.3 as spellings using the look – cover – write – check procedure (see Chapter Nine) and memorize difficult bits such as ' – ough' as spelling patterns. It may help Robin to learn phonic 'chunks' as described on page 69 but this might reinforce his habit of vocalizing sounds. It is therefore important to make sure that Robin practises new words until they are read fluently and without hesitation.

> Jane: 'He could not s... for he was hot. The children tired to,
>   too tired pull him as ...'
> Text: He could not swim for he was hurt. The children
>   tried to pull him ashore.

Teacher's notes: Jane relies almost entirely on sight words and tries to make some sense of the story. Her phonic knowledge is weak, e.g. sw in 'swim', ur in 'hurt', tr in 'tried'. *Action:* Check blends and digraphs using the phonic checklist described below and follow the methods of teaching described on page 68. Reassess Jane's performance on a more interesting text.

A phonic checklist for Stage III

The checklists in Table 8.1 will help you assess which phonic structures have already been mastered. The lists are not all inclusive; other checklists introduce letter combinations not mentioned here and vary the order in which the phonic rules are presented (see for example Jackson's *Phonic Checklist*, described on page 11, or Cotterel's *Checklist of Basic Sounds* (1973, listed in the Resources page at the back of this manual). You can make up your own checklists based on the phonic teaching materials available to you. Our subdivision of phonics into stages is also arbitrary in that there is no real cut-off point between Stages II, III and IV. For example, words with the short medial vowel at Stage II (e.g. 'cat') lead easily to words with a short medial vowel at Stage III (e.g. 'spot').

The lists of words in Table 8.1, have been ordered roughly according to level of difficulty so that it is assumed that words from List A and List B are easier than the lists that follow. The words in the later lists also build on the skills learnt earlier, for example, List D includes consonant blends and digraphs which should have been mastered at List A or B level.

The checklists in Table 8.1 can be used in the following ways:

(a) Hear the pupil read his book. Write down words which cause difficulty and categorize them by referring to the checklist. You can use copies of Table 8.1 as the pupil's individual record form and check off the types of letter combinations he clearly copes with, while making a note of those which will need further practice. Alternatively, you can design your own record form, if you find that Table 8.1 gives you insufficient space.

(b) Use the words which illustrate each list as a criterion-referenced test. Take List A as an example. Make up a set of cards by printing one of the words on each card. As the pupil reads the words, the cards can be placed in three piles: cards read with ease, those read correctly but slowly and those read incorrectly. If the pupil reads a word correctly but slowly, listen carefully to the strategy used in sounding out the word. It is essential that pupils read blends and digraphs as one sound unit; if they sound out a word letter by letter, their strategy is faulty and they need to learn a better way. Write down what the pupils read when they misread a word. You may find, for example, that they read the initial consonant blend correctly but confuse the medial vowel. Use Table 8.1 as a record of the pupil's performance noting which words were read with ease, which were read slowly, therefore indicating a need for some more practice of that blend, and which misreadings demonstrate a need for more extensive help.

(c) You could assume that if children can spell a word correctly, then they can also blend the sounds in it. Therefore, you might use the words in Table 8.1 as graded spelling tests to identify those pupils who have difficulties. This has the additional advantage of enabling you to test the whole class at once if necessary.

Table 8.1:
Phonic checklist for Stage III

List A	Initial consonant blends:		st br dr fr gr pr tr cr bl cl fl gl pl sl sm sn sp sk sw tw	

pram	glad	spot	step
trip	plot	skip	bring
blot	slip	crab	drip
clap	smell	swim	frog
flip	snap	twig	grass

List B	Final consonant blends:	st nd ng lt mp sk lk ft nk nt
	Consonant digraphs:	ch sh th

rest	lamp	shop	this
milk	hand	chip	rush
desk	ring	think	chest
lift	mint	ship	with
belt	sink	rich	wish

List C	Triple initial blends:	scr shr spl spr str
	Vowel digraphs:	ee oo ea er ou

spring	peel	week	keep
scrap	boot	moon	food
splash	speak	team	meat
strong	sister	winter	number
shrimp	loud	sound	shout

List D	Vowel digraphs:	ir ur ow ai ay ar

cow	first	sail	mark
shirt	stay	bird	crown
train	arm	start	spray
burn	burst	church	
down	wait	pay	

List E	Vowel digraphs:	aw or oi oy
	Silent 'e':	a...e i...e

draw	ride	shine	annoy
boil	coin	lawn	smile
gate	game	point	straw
fork	short	shake	
toy	enjoy	sport	

List F	Vowel digraphs:	oa au ie ew
	Silent 'e':	o...e u...e

stone	new	chief	excuse
soap	rose	stew	brief
author	roast	bone	chew
tune	laundry	coat	
thief	cube	Paul	

2. Teaching materials

Once you have identified the child's needs at Stage III, appropriate materials, including games, can be obtained from a number of sources mentioned in the Bibliography. Words which illustrate the phonic structures can be found in the NARE publication *A Classroom Index of Phonic Resources* (Herbert and Davies-Jones, 1983), which is updated regularly – see Resources page at the end of this manual.

There is usually no need to repeat long lists of words to illustrate a particular 'rule'; a few sample words are considered sufficient. Ideally these words should be taken from the pupil's reading book or reading scheme so that we can encourage transfer of training to ordinary reading practice. This can be achieved by making up a chart as illustrated in Table 8.2 (page 71). Here, some of the letter combinations which occur in 'Griffin Pirate Readers' One to Three (Arnold) have been extracted and example words provided for each. The numbers in the corner of each subheading refer to the book from which the first sample word was taken. A few extra words are added to each list bearing in mind that these words should not include phonics at a more difficult level. You can make up your own charts based on the approximate reading level of the book and the learning needs of the pupil. A further example is provided in Table 8.3 which also includes a section for listing new sight words which do not conform to any regular phonic pattern. The content of Table 8.2 can easily be transferred onto a set of cards for teaching purposes.

3. Methods of teaching

(a) For initial and final consonant blends and digraphs (Lists A, B and half of C) you can follow the procedure outlined in Stage II page 55 for word building. This involves adding plastic letters or letters written on small cards to the beginning or to the end of a medial vowel. For example:

Final blends	*Initial blends*
la – nd	cha – t
la – sh	fla – t
la – mp	bra – t
la – st	tha – t
la – ck	sla – t
la – tch	spra – t

Make sure that blends are always pronounced as one unit and that the initial blend merges with the subsequent vowel (e.g. cri – sp). This may need lengthy practice involving short lists of 'cue' words written on cards and, sometimes, 'clue' pictures (see below).

(b) Initial cue practice in context: Initial consonant blends and digraphs can be learnt during reading practice. The teacher scans ahead, identifies an appropriate word towards the end of a sentence and covers up all but the initial blend and vowel of the word (e.g. chi...). The pupil then sounds the blend and 'guesses' the word from context.

(c) A few pupils need more extensive practice using similar

methods to those outlined under Stage II for single letter sounds. The learning sequence starts from a picture cue, then introduces word cues and finally the pupil is required to give an automatic response to the blend or digraph. For example:

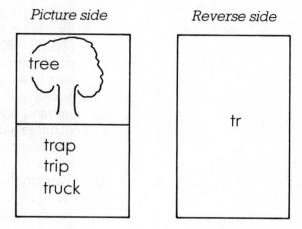

Picture side   *Reverse side*

tree

trap
trip
truck

tr

The pupil first names the picture and says the initial blend. He then reads the sample words underneath. After that he turns over the card and says the blend once more in isolation.

As at Stage II, the pupil might like to choose his own picture cues and draw them. Introducing a few cards at a time, the 'quick flip' exercise (see page 54) is practised until the recognition of the blends on the reverse side becomes automatic. The pupil eventually has his own set of flashcards with examples of those Stage III blends and vowel digraphs which he has needed to learn. Even when the cards have been mastered, the pupil should go over them from time to time to ensure continued automatic recall. Older pupils may find it useful to carry a small, pocket-sized learning pack of cards which they can produce for practice at odd moments.

(d) Many children can manage without the picture cue and only need a few sample words taken, whenever possible, from the reading book. The content of Table 8.2 can be converted to this form. Each card in the set would look like this:

Front   *Reverse*

ee

see
tree
green
three

ee

The pupils learn to read the front of the card quickly and easily. They then practise the recognition of the isolated blend on the reverse of the card using the 'quick flip' method.

(e) Dictation of words and sentences which illustrate the use of the letter combinations is often recommended in conjunction with the reading drill. For example, Hornsby and Shear (1980) suggest that after the pupil has said the sound of the printed blend, he should be able to write the letters when the sound is said by the teacher. It should be noted that many written phonic exercises (e.g. filling in missing words, matching or marking the odd one out) are of little real value as they do not require the speedy verbal response needed in reading.

(f) The single most natural method of learning phonics is through reading practice where relevant phonic cues are noticed and used whenever necessary. It can help to keep the set of cue cards at hand and refer to the appropriate card as to a dictionary. The pupil's motivation can be enhanced by 'catching' him using a recently learnt phonic cue and praising him for doing so.

Table 8.2
Words from a reading scheme

th	gr	bl	ee	ea
1	1	1	1	1
the	green	black	three	each
that	grass	blue	see	sea
this	grin		tree	read
path			green	

ch	oo	ay	cr	sh
1	1	1	1	1
each	boots	away	across	ship
chip	too	say	cross	push
chin	moon	way		shone
		lay		she
		always		

fl	ai	or	ow (2)	sk
1	1	1	1	3
flag	sail	for	flower	sky
flower	nail	forget	how	skip
	afraid	storm	brown	
			know	
			blow	

ur	ar	aw	st	ing
3	3	3	3	3
purple	far	saw	still	sing
turn	part	claw	stop	ring
	art	draw		sailing
	hard			digging

ew	er	ou	all	oo
3	3	3	3	3
blew	hotter	out	all	shook
knew	mother	loudly	fall	look
few	never	found	tall	took
	perhaps			

Table 8.3:
Chart for phonic classification of
words from a specified reading book

sh	ch	wh	qu	th	ph	
ar	or	er	ir	ur	oi	oy
a–e	i–e	o–e	u–e	ou	ow	oo
ee	ea	ea	oa	ai	ay	y
ie	oe	ue	ew		Compound words	Poly-syllabic words

Sight words:

The Stage IV reader

The teaching methods described for Stage III are also used at Stage IV. However, it is a matter of opinion as to how many of the more unusual and/or complex phonic structures should be taught. We prefer to teach the very minimum, as we believe that pupils who have reached this stage can progress as a result of reading practice alone. The words causing difficulty in the context of reading can then be used as a starting point for further discussion and analysis. Instead of memorizing 'rules' we would recommend more opportunities for repetition as described in Chapter Five. For these reasons we make no apology for excluding many phonic structures from the checklist in Table 8.4. If you think that the individual pupil continues to need a highly structured phonic approach even at this stage, you can consult, for example, *Alpha to Omega* (Hornsby and Shear, 1980) for more details.

Silent letters and longer word endings

The letter combinations represented by List A and List B in Table 8.4 can be taught in a similar manner to those at Stage III. A few words exemplifying each 'rule' are written on cards and the pupil learns to read the set of cards fluently.

Table 8.4:
Phonic checklist for Stage IV

List A	Silent letters: w k b h u c		
	write	scent	builder	biscuit
	knife	sword	scissors	scene
	lamb	knot	answer	
	ghost	bomb	knee	
	guard	rhyme	plumber	

List B	Longer word endings: tion sion ture ous ious		
	picture	furniture	adventure
	attention	education	question
	permission	discussion	impression
	dangerous	marvellous	enormous
	suspicious	unconscious	delicious

Continued overleaf

List C   Compound words:

birthday	rainbow
seatbelt	roundabout
policeman	lifeboat
sandpaper	knowledge
sunlight	peacock
gentleman	beetroot
handsome	cheesecake
workshop	strawberry
anywhere	wallflower
blackboard	countryside

List D   Polysyllabic words:

attractive	telephone
impossible	photograph
automatic	completely
wonderful	explanation
comfortable	economic
embroidery	confidence
atmosphere	introduce
surprise	remember
raspberry	develop
certificate	addition

Compound words

Some pupils may not have learnt that many long words are made up of two short and relatively easy words. List C helps you to check this. Although compound words have been allocated to Stage IV, they should have been introduced incidentally at an earlier stage with examples such as 'postman', 'milkman', 'dustman', 'dustbin', 'dustpan'. Words taken from the context of meaningful reading make the best examples. When learning to read compound words, a few pupils may find it helpful to underline lightly each of the short words involved.

Polysyllabic words

List D gives some examples. In deciphering a polysyllabic word out of context, the pupil has to be able to look for manageable sound units, to merge these units and to guess the rest (for example, wond – er – ful, cert – if – ic – ate, ex – plan – a – tion). For the purpose of practice it is helpful to attempt to underline the sound units first. It is obviously very contrived to learn unknown words out of their meaningful context and we prefer to teach such words as they are encountered when the pupil reads a book. This means that compound words and polysyllables are introduced quite early on, as soon as they appear in the reading scheme. Children can enjoy the challenge of trying to read and write such words, particularly as they find that the words are really only made up of quite easy elements, e.g. hipp – o – pot – am – us.

Long word jigsaws are also a popular way of teaching polysyllables. Made according to the instructions below, they reinforce the skills of analysis. It is important to ensure that the child scans the words from left to right. Since the words are not cut into syllables, pieces cannot be lost or words confused.

Long word jigsaws

(a) Children make their own examples taken from their reading.

(b) Use thin card, approximately 15cm × 7cm. Fold it longitudinally.

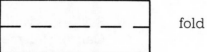 fold

(c) The word is written boldly on the lower half of the card. The syllables are marked lightly in pencil with the line extending to the top half of the card.

(d) Cut through the top half of the card to make up flaps which cover each syllable.

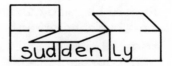

(e) Syllables are revealed from left to right one at a time.

Learning phonic skills in context

This method of teaching encourages the child to use phonics to check contextual guesses. By locating difficult words and working out strategies for reading them, the pupil is helped to take responsibility for the reading practice. The procedure is summarized below.

(a) Let the child read the story or passage to you while you supply the unfamiliar words; the first 'read' is for content only without emphasis on phonics.

(b) Talk about the content before starting word analysis.

(c)   Ask the child to find the difficult word, i.e. a word previously supplied by the teacher. Read the whole sentence again and pronounce the unknown word slowly and clearly.

(d)   Ask, 'How could you have worked that out if I hadn't told you?' A good answer would refer to context and word structure, e.g. 'It must be "bridge" because it says "over the river" and it starts with br'.

(e)   Say, 'How will you know this word next time you see it? Can you tell me how it is made?' 'Yes, br – i – dge.' 'Let's think of some more words with – dge.' Write them in the pupil's reading notebook:
        badge   ledge   fudge   ridge   judge   wedge

      'Read the words.' 'Where is the tricky bit?' 'See if you can cover up the words and write them as I say them.'

(f)   As the words have been entered in the pupil's reading notebook, they can be returned to regularly until the pupil can read and write them automatically.

(g)   A similar procedure is followed when teaching compound words and polysyllabic words.

(h)   Useful lists of words can be found in the NARE publication *A Classroom Index of Phonic Resources* (Herbert and Davies-Jones, 1983; see Resources page at the end of this manual) which is updated regularly. Long lists are not recommended; just a few sample words to illustrate the phonic structure.

Record keeping

Record keeping can follow the principles already outlined in previous chapters and illustrated, for example, by Table 7.2 on page 59. The teacher subdivides a skill area into specified targets, or 'steps', sets a standard (e.g. a 'score') which indicates when the target has been learnt and then makes checks at later dates to ensure that the skill or the knowledge has been retained. It is important to include a heading for noting when a particular skill is applied in ordinary reading or writing activities and not only during lessons which the pupil knows relate to phonics. To enhance motivation to learn, it is also essential to involve the pupil in the record keeping. A daily chart can be useful: the pupil gives a tick to those words or letter sounds read/written correctly and then gives the task a 'score' for the day (e.g. 12 out of 15). The teacher should always include enough mastered or nearly mastered items in the list so that the pupil can achieve a respectable 'score'. Further practice of those items which caused difficulty should then ensure that increasingly higher 'scores' are achieved on subsequent days.

Conclusion

We have argued that phonics should be taught as an integral part of a language-based reading programme and not as an isolated skill. At first, the pupil with difficulties needs a carefully graded approach. She will need to learn that letters stand for sounds, that when these are put together they make words which have a meaning and that 'word building' is only applied to a word which cannot be recognized in other ways, such as by its shape, initial letters and within its context.

Our views and suggestions in this section can be summarized in the form of a number of 'principles' for learning phonics:

(a) Teach phonics in parallel with enhanced opportunities for word recognition as described in Chapters Five and Six. Our aim is to foster easy and effortless reading, not over-reliance on word by word analysis of the text.

(b) There is usually no need to practise long lists of words which illustrate phonic structures. The pupil should learn to read a few words containing the particular structure and then be helped to apply the rule to new words during normal reading practice. We consider the teaching of complex or unusual rules a waste of time.

(c) We have argued that inability to learn phonics incidentally can be caused by difficulties in retaining the auditory representations of the visual symbols. Mnemonic aids in the form of cue pictures or cue words should be of help here.

(d) Teach memory drills step by step during frequent short sessions, always ensuring mastery for each learning step. The learner should aim for speedy and automatic recognition of sound units and/or whole words.

(e) It is essential that the pupil learns to isolate and blend sound units and does not acquire the ineffective habit of attempting to 'read' a word letter by letter.

(f) Recognition is easier than recall. We may, for example, not be able to remember the name of a person but when the name is mentioned to us, we instantly recognize its owner. The same principle applies to reading. Therefore, the learning sequence should consist of the teacher first saying a word or sound unit and the pupil finding its written representation. Only when the pupil can recognize the word or sound unit is she required to recall it for herself.

(g) The principle of active learning tells us that repetition alone does not help the pupil learn. We may, for example, repeat passively a word 100 times but if we do not actively look for strategies of memorizing or employ self-testing procedures, it is unlikely that we will have benefited from the exercise.

(h) There is a close link between reading and writing practice when learning about phonic regularities. Only when the pupil can spell the relevant words has she demonstrated that she has really learnt the phonic structures.

(i) Much of written English is not phonetically regular. It is vital that we teach for diversity and encourage an approach based on flexible guesswork.

(j) The pupil should always feel able to complete the learning successfully. Tasks which involve memory or the integration of automatic responses (such as learning to drive a car) are performed significantly better when we feel confident. It is essential that the pupil and the teacher share a sense of progress, and, also, a sense of fun.

(k) Records of progress will indicate exactly what reading stage the child has reached and which phonic structures she is in the process of learning. When listening to the child read, the skilled teacher is able to provide appropriate prompts based on that information.

Chapter 9   Spelling

Introduction

Spelling differs from reading in that it requires accurate perception and reproduction of sequences of letters which cannot be guessed from the context. Children who have specific learning difficulties in reading almost inevitably find spelling a problem. In addition, there are many average or good readers whose spelling is weak.

The procedure outlined in Chapters Seven and Eight is intended to establish the learning of regular words in both spelling and reading. It would be undesirable, however, even if it were possible, for children to limit their written expression to phonically regular words. In this section, therefore, we also discuss the words children need to practise in their writing.

Although spelling is a different kind of activity from reading, most of the principles outlined in previous chapters still apply. In spelling, however, it is not possible, as in reading, to compensate for weaknesses with strengths. Poor spellers who have to rely on their strengths resort to writing short pieces with a limited vocabulary of easy words. As a result their weaknesses do not come to light, and progress is minimal.

Similarly, in spelling as compared to reading the use of context is limited to enabling us to differentiate between homophones: e.g. 'there' or 'their'.

Motivation and success

Failure in spelling is tantamount to failure in written communication. This leads to unwillingness to write, lack of practice in accurate spelling, and further failure. Before he can begin to break out of this cycle, the child needs the prospect of success. We must, therefore, define clear principles in the teaching of spelling and establish positive attitudes. These may be stated as follows:

1. Accurate spelling matters. It gives children confidence to express themselves as they wish.

2. Self-esteem in spelling is important. Children who label themselves poor spellers have already admitted defeat. It is more positive to say, 'I have to work hard at my spellings, but I know these words'.

3. The teacher's feelings about words can colour the attitude of the whole class. If spelling is regarded as an irritating nuisance and errors as punishable carelessness, poor spellers will learn to hate writing. If, on the other hand, the impression is conveyed that words are intriguing and exciting, the children are more likely to catch this enthusiasm and work hard at their spelling.

4. Learning how to learn spellings is a skill in itself which

should be taught. It is not the same as learning lists of words.

5. The will to learn to spell and the habit of looking at words 'with intent' to memorize the sequence of letters are both essential to success.

6. Time should be set aside in school for learning spellings. If work is to be done at home, parents must be instructed in the teaching procedures to be adopted, emphasizing encouragement and enjoyment, correct learning processes, and short intense periods of practice.

7. It is easy to learn to spell inaccurately. Consistent misspelling of the same word reinforces the mistake each time it is written. Repeated inaccurate copying from a textbook (e.g. a maths book) may be the source of such erroneous learning, for example:

$$3 \times 4 = 12 \text{ because } 4 \times 3 = 12$$
$$2 \times 6 = 12 \text{ because } 6 \times 2 = 12 \text{ etc.}$$

Assessment and programme planning

Normative assessment is of limited value in indicating a child's spelling ability. A standardized score does not tell us which words children would *like* to write, but avoid because they cannot spell them. It gives little diagnostic information about what the child's difficulties are.

Children's own written work gives clues to their spelling problems. Patterns of misspelling fall into two major categories, the visual and the phonic. These may be compared to the categories in Table 4.1 'Stages in Learning to Read' (page 14).

The evidence from their writing often suggests that children have some simple phonic knowledge but that it does not go far enough. Those with reading difficulties who are following the 'Phonics' programme should be learning to spell the same regular words. Other poor spellers, who do not need such highly structured phonics teaching to help with their reading, may still benefit from a systematic 'mastery' approach to phonics – for – spelling.

Children who have a poor visual memory often make quite unpredictable spelling errors, even to the extent of being inconsistent in their mistakes. Sometimes they are incapable of reading their own work. Such children need extensive drill with the same words using the 'look – cover – write – check' technique described below, and any other aids which prove helpful. A case of severe spelling difficulties is discussed at the end of this chapter.

Learning how to learn spellings

The technique of learning spellings is not usually acquired incidentally. It has to be taught. Traditional methods like copying out spellings a set number of times, or spelling out alphabetically, are grossly inefficient. Most good spellers know when a word **looks** right, and this is the skill that we want children to develop. The method described in Table 9.1 can help all children to improve their spelling, not only those who are experiencing difficulty.

Table 9.1:
Learning to spell

1.	LOOK	at the word with the intention of remembering it. Pronounce it carefully. Are there any tricky bits? What clues will help you to remember it?
2.	COVER	the word and think the spelling.
3.	WRITE	it correctly and without hesitating. Does it look right?
4.	CHECK	that it is right.

Repeat the process until you are sure of the word.

This technique should be used for new spellings, for corrections, and for copying words from a reference source. That is, children should try to remember the whole word, not copy letter by letter. A favourite way to practise this procedure is to write each word at the top of a strip of paper (half the width of an exercise page). After studying it the child folds the word out of sight, and attempts to write it. Checking is done by unfolding the paper. At the end of several practices the paper is folded over and over as in the game of 'Consequences' with the word written on each space.

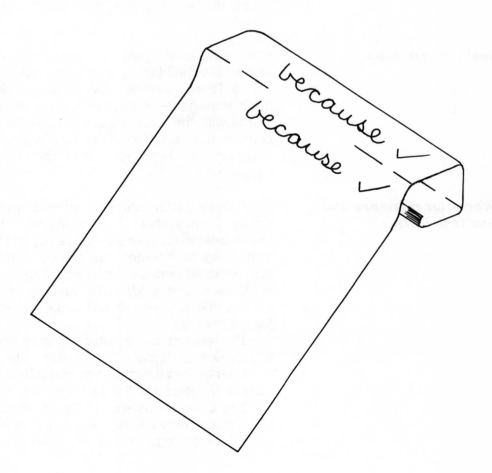

Handwriting

An essential feature of the 'look – cover – write – check' learning procedure is to be able to write the spelling unhesitatingly and clearly. In order to do this, it is necessary for the child to have a fluent and accurate handwriting style. The relevance of handwriting to spelling is discussed more fully in Chapter Ten.

'Non-phonic' sources of error

Even moderately competent spellers sometimes make mistakes, not because of inadequate knowledge of phonic conventions, but for a variety of reasons which may include the following:

1. *Homophone confusion* (e.g. 'their' and 'there'). This should be approached by teaching the words separately in accordance with usage. 'There' goes with 'here' and 'where'. 'Their' is like 'our' and 'your'.

2. *Mispronunciations.* 'Stopport' for Stockport and 'libry' for library can be corrected by pronouncing each syllable distinctly.

3. *Fear of long words.* When children realize that long words can be broken into easy syllables, learning the spelling becomes much simpler. Accurate reading and meticulous pronunciation of the syllables helps to ensure success.

Copying

As noted earlier, children often make mistakes when copying from a textbook or from the teacher's writing and consequently learn wrong spellings. The 'look – cover – write – check' procedure should be practised even for the short-term memorizing required for copying a word. By this means the child attempts to remember the whole word and takes care to check that it is right.

Spelling textbooks

Many published 'spelling programmes' require children to insert words into blanks, to untangle anagrams or to find missing letters. These easily degenerate into mechanical exercises, but, more important, do not encourage children to look at whole words with the intention of learning them. Indeed, anagrams confuse the visual recall of words. All such texts should be carefully evaluated to ensure that they fulfil the intended purpose.

Words for reference and words to learn

Poor spelling often inhibits children from writing what they wish to say. Even without this self-imposed restraint, it would be unreasonable for teachers to restrict children's written expression to words that they can spell correctly. We therefore advise establishing an easy-to-use reference system of common spellings so that children can find the words they need. It is important that children should make the effort to find the words for themselves.

The teacher can construct a 'core vocabulary' of 100 – 200 words most in demand by the class. These might constitute 50 to 70 per cent of the spellings normally needed. Our own compilation is offered in Table 9.2 at the end of this chapter.

The core words should be physically accessible by the child, so that they can be taken to his table for study. The words might be affixed to a chart, or stored in a box as a Word Bank, in either case in alphabetical order. Where a Language Master is available, words can be written on the special cards so that children may check their selection by listening to it. As in other copying, the 'look – cover – write – check' procedure should be followed.

A personal alphabetic word-book is a necessary adjunct to the class reference list. In this the child can attempt words to see if they look right, or if necessary, ask the teacher to write the spellings required. If the child records in it words as they are needed, the book can be a source of learning tasks in spelling. Longmans ('Breakthrough') publish a word-book with many useful spellings already printed, and space for more.

Dictionaries

Topic-dictionaries like *My Word* (Schofield and Sims) and picture-dictionaries are useful aids for some spellings, but an ordinary dictionary is not. The writer must have a reasonable idea of how a word begins before being able to make good use of a dictionary for checking spellings, and poor spellers find this difficult.

It is important, however, that every child should be familiar with standard dictionaries and their usage. All kinds of reference games can be played with a dictionary, so that children may handle it with confidence, for example:

1. On what page do letter B words begin?
2. What is the last word for letter Y?
3. On what page does the word 'king' appear?

(Note that you may have to teach the child to recite the alphabet first.)

Words to learn

Writers learn most readily those words they use frequently, both because motivation is enhanced and because practice in real situations is more effective than mechanical drill. 'Phonic families' have more immediacy if the starting-point is a word needed by the child in writing. A request for the spelling of 'work', for example, might subsequently be followed by study of 'word', 'world', 'worm', 'worse'.

Testing

It is not difficult to test a class on their individual spelling lists. All that is necessary is to have children dictating the words to each other. The teacher then marks the tests. Children may enter the score on their own bar-charts and follow their weekly progress without undesirable competition.

Rules

Spelling rules are essential if writers are to systematize their learning, but complex rules of the 'i before e' variety are often impossibly difficult for children. The best rules and mnemonics are those devised by learners themselves, such as 'a piece of pie' or deliberate 'phonic' mispronunciation: 'k – now, beca – use.'

Many published spelling schemes give basic rules, but they are not always expressed in a way that poor spellers can understand. Whatever the source of the rule, to be effective it must be accompanied by an example which the child should learn.

Marking and corrections

When children wish to express themselves in writing, they cannot give equal attention to ideas and to spelling, punctuation and presentation. The teacher does not want to cover their work in red ink, and yet as it stands the writing may be incomprehensible. There is no single solution to this problem, but the following suggestions might be taken into account:

1. The teacher should consider whether an alternative means of expression is possible, e.g. using a tape recorder or 'Breakthrough sentence maker' or writing to the child's dictation.

2. The purpose of the writing affects the standards required by the teacher. Where the child is recording facts recently learned, time can be taken to ensure that the spelling is correct in the first instance. Where the writing is more creative, however, it is often necessary to accept spelling errors which may subsequently be erased and corrected either by the child or by the teacher.

3. Occasionally, work which is interesting in content but poorly presented can be typed or written out correctly by the teacher so that the child knows that the value of the ideas has been recognized.

4. Children should have the marking system explained. Unless the teacher makes it clear that all the errors have not been marked, the child will probably assume that unmarked words are correct.

5. The marking of spelling mistakes which are not to be corrected is negative and depressing to the child. The teacher should either write the word correctly, ask the child to correct and learn it, or ignore the error.

6. Sometimes a child's writing is required for 'publication' and must be meticulously corrected. Usually, however, corrections to a piece of work should not be extensive.

7. The purpose of doing spelling corrections to a piece of writing should be to learn thoroughly a limited number of words. This is to be seen, not as a punishment for carelessness, but as a development from the writing.

8. Children should form the habit of reading through their work on finishing it, so that eventually they learn to check for errors. Poor spellers cannot be expected to be good at self-editing, but they can be given specific checking tasks to do. For example, if b/d confusion is a problem, the child can provide himself with a 'bed' reference card (see below) and award himself a tick for every b and d written correctly, erasing and correcting the others. If this can be turned into a game, so much the better. In checking on the word 'was', for example, the child could act as a detective and search all the written examples of the word to make sure that no misspellings have crept in. This approach has the further advantage of transferring blame from the child to the 'naughty word'.

search card

Spelling tasks and tests

It has been suggested above that children should be learning the spellings they most need, and that testing can be done by other children on a one-to-one basis. The more responsibility children take for selecting their own spelling tasks, the more successful learning is likely to be.

Spelling tests are generally regarded as assessment procedures for the teacher, but children's interest in assessing their perceived learning is also important. The poor speller especially needs the reassurance of success. Weekly spelling tasks and tests must, therefore, avoid presenting too much of a challenge. The number of words to be learnt must be within the child's capabilities. Matching the work to the child in this way results in different tasks for different children. One might learn twenty new words in a week and remember them permanently. Another might do well to memorize two words each day, and require frequent repetition of the same tasks for many weeks before they can be said to be mastered. For such a child it is advisable to include in the weekly list some words which are already known. This not only ensures that the test score is respectable, it also provides an opportunity to consolidate previous learning.

Suggestions for helping a poor speller

Richard, aged eight and a half, has been a late beginner in reading. He does not look carefully at the details of words and reads, for example, 'When I grow up' for 'When I am big'. He has difficulty in controlling his pencil, but manages to form letters correctly on the whole. His writing is usually brief and laboured. He makes very few requests for spellings.

An unusually long story written by Richard is reproduced below. At first sight it appears incomprehensible. Indeed, Richard himself was unable to read it without help the day after he wrote it. By working together, however, the teacher and Richard recalled what he had intended. The teacher said how much she had enjoyed the story and promised to type it out for him.

A careful analysis of Richard's story reveals that he is not without some spelling ability. He knows some words and makes a 'phonic' attempt at the others. A spelling programme based on his errors is devised. The story itself remains unmarked apart from a comment by the teacher on the content.

Wednesday, 27th April

Title: Aliens are Invading

In the deep of space other forms of life are watching us ready to take over.

At night a cylinder passed over the village. Next day the village people ran to the cylinder. (The) top opened. A huge iron eye came out of the cylinder. Then a leather body came out. It killed people and it went to the station. And I had a rest in my home (waiting) for a ship. I went into a ship. I saw a light. The world is blown up.

Richard's spelling programme

Since Richard lags far behind his classmates in spelling, he needs his own individual spelling programme. An analysis of his story prompts these observations:

Strengths
1. Some idea of phonic rules: 'day', 'home', 'nite'.
2. An ability to generate spelling rules, albeit inaccurate: 'titul' (title), 'pepul' (people); 'redea' (ready), 'bodea' (body).
3. An attempt at the words he needs: 'silind' (cylinder), 'stachn' (station).

Weaknesses
1. Poor visual retention even of spellings on view: 'Wedsday' (Wednesday) copied from the blackboard.
2. Inconsistent errors: 'kam'/'cam' (came).
3. Misspellings of some of the commonest words: 'ov' (of), 'att' (at), 'sor' (saw).

In order to sustain Richard's interest in the task, his spelling programme is initially based on words from the story. To these the teacher adds further examples belonging to the same spelling family and taken mostly from the 'Basic Spelling Vocabulary' (Table 9.2).

Words are introduced in phonic family sets of four or five. The aim is to enable Richard to generate rules, and associate similar words with each other. A list of fewer than four words might not provide enough evidence from which to generate rules.

The first few sets are as follows:

1.	ready*	2.	ready*	3.	other*	4.	other*	5.	huge*
	head		body*		another		over*		tube
	dead		nobody		mother		ever		rule
	leather*		very		brother		after		blue

* asterisked words are from the story

With the help of his teacher, Richard is expected to identify the 'tricky bits' of each set, and to say, but not write, which rule is operating, for example:

Set 1: 'ea' represents short e.
Set 2: A final short i sound is written 'y'
Set 3: All the words end in '–other'. The letter 'o' is used to represent short u.
Set 4: The letters 'er' sound like uh.
Set 5: Magic 'e' makes u say its name.

It will be noted that the same words are repeated in different lists where attention is being focused on another phonic element in the word.

Some of the words listed may be outside Richard's reading sight vocabulary or beyond his level of phonic learning. This is not important. The words he is to learn to spell are those he has already demonstrated a need for in his story or they are commonly used words from Table 9.2 which he is likely to need. When he can spell them he will be able to read them.

Learning and testing

Richard needs a variety of materials for learning his spellings. He keeps them in a plastic wallet. They consist of:

– A small narrow notebook in which the teacher writes each set of words to be learned, and records progress.
– A similar notebook for tests.
– An exercise book in which to write sentences.
– Strips of scrap paper for practice.

Richard learns the 'Look – Cover – Write – Check' procedure. Each time he is ready for a new set of words, he and the teacher read the new words together from the teacher's record book. They discuss the 'tricky bits' and formulate a rule. Richard then practises the words on scrap paper until he is sure of them. Next he gets a friend to dictate the words to him from the teacher's record book. The teacher marks the test.

The standard, or criterion, of mastery is to score all correct (100 per cent) in tests on four successive days. Further checks on the same words are made after intervals of one and two weeks. In addition, Richard tests himself by writing a sentence containing some of the words practised. There must be no errors in the sentence. A sentence is written every day when no new words are being introduced.

The sequence of learning tasks in Richard's test book is listed below. To save space here, the words have been written horizontally; in the test book they are listed vertically so that there is space for entering dates and ticks as a record of progress.

Day 1:	ready, head, dead, leather (new words)
Day 2:	head, ready, leather, dead
Day 3:	leather, dead, ready, head + new set: ready, body, nobody, very
Day 4:	head, ready, dead, leather, body, very, nobody
Day 5:	body, ready, very, nobody Introduce sentence writing: 'The dead body had no head but nobody was ready to find it.'
Day 6:	body, very, ready, nobody + sentence
Day 7:	nobody, ready, body, very + new set: other, another, mother, brother
Day 8:	another, mother, brother, other + sentence
Day 9:	brother, another, other, mother + sentence
Day 10:	Composite test: head, body, other, very, mother, ready, nobody, brother, leather, another, dead.

New words are added to the list only when previous ones have been learnt. Composite tests are given every Friday.

Record keeping

The test book and sentence book are records of Richard's success. In addition, each time he gets a whole set of words right in a composite test, he is allowed to stamp the date on the appropriate page of the teacher's record book using the school library rubber stamp. This ensures that a check is kept on retention and, at the same time, rewards Richard by allowing him the rare privilege of using the stamp.

Comment

The above approach is given in some detail but should be adapted to the individual child. The words selected should be those relevant to the child, and the number of words presented together should be adapted to the individual's rate of learning. Similarly, the amount of repetition and the number of tests for each set of words must be modified to ensure success. When setting up an individual spelling programme it is important to ensure that:

1. The child always practises 'Look – Cover – Write – Check'.
2. Learning targets are words which the child is likely to need.
3. Words are presented in sets to facilitate associations based on letter-strings.
4. There is provision for ample repetition and testing at increasing intervals of time.
5. Once the routine has been established, testing and record keeping are simple and automatic.

In order to ensure that the learning is being transferred to 'real' writing, Richard looks through his written work for the words he is learning, awarding ticks to the correct ones and erasing those words which have 'spelled themselves wrongly'. The amount of writing he does is at this stage restricted. He reads it aloud as soon as he has finished, either to the teacher or to a friend, and whenever possible it is copied for him and a correct version put in his book. Richard's handwriting and spacing also need attention as described in the next chapter.

Summary

By giving a detailed analysis of one piece of writing, we hope to have demonstrated a method of beginning to teach spelling to a child with severe difficulties. The important aspects of this approach may be summarized as follows:

1. The teacher showed that she valued the content of the story.
2. She analysed what Richard could do, in addition to his errors.
3. No corrections were asked.
4. Richard took some responsibility for checking his own work.
5. Parents and friends were able to help with the learning and checking.

Table 9.2:
Basic spelling vocabulary

A	**C**	father	holiday	love
about	called	find	hospital	
across	came	finish	house	**M**
after	can't	first	how	made
afternoon	car	for	home	make
again	catch	found		many
all	children	friend	**I**	may
always	Christmas	from	if	me
and	come	front	into	minute
another	could			money
and		**G**	**J**	morning
are	**D**	game	just	mother
ask	daddy	gave		Mr
auntie	day	girl	**K**	Mrs
away	do	give	keep	much
	does	go	kept	mummy
B	doesn't	goes	knew	must
baby	don't	going	know	my
back	down	good		
because	draw	grandma	**L**	**N**
been			ladies	name
before	**E**	**H**	lady	near
behind	each	had	last	never
best	eat	hadn't	learn	new
birthday	end	have	left	next
boy	ever	head	like	nice
bring	every	help	little	night
brother		her	live	nobody
brought	**F**	here	look	nothing
buy	family	high	looked	now
by	far	his	lost	nowhere

O	**R**	than	**V**	won't
o'clock	ready	thank	very	work
of	right	that		worked
off	round	the	**W**	would
old	running	their	walk	wouldn't
once		them	walked	write
one	**S**	then	want	writing
only	said	there	wanted	
open	same	they	was	**Y**
other	saw	thing	watch	year
or	say	think	watched	yes
our	school	this	water	yesterday
out	she	those	way	you
over	should	thought	we	your
own	sister	through	week	
	slow	time	went	
P	so	to	were	
people	soon	today	what	
picture	stay	told	when	
place	stopped	too	where	
play	stopping	two	which	
please	street		while	
police		**U**	who	
	T	uncle	why	
Q	take	under	will	
quick	taking	use	wish	
quickly	talk	used	wished	
quiet	teacher	using	woman	
quite	television		women	

Simple two and three letter words have been omitted but could be added for younger or less able children (e.g. is, at, on, but).

Colours, numbers, days of the week, months of the year could be inserted or stored in classified lists.

Chapter 10   Handwriting

Introduction

Good handwriting is neither as important nor as complex as fluent reading and accurate spelling. Ultimately the problem of poor handwriting can be solved by learning to type. Nevertheless, the ability to write legibly and easily is valued in school, partly because careful presentation enhances the content of written work. There are, however, other reasons why children should learn to write well. Amongst the most important are these:

1. Properly formed handwriting is quicker than versions created spontaneously by children themselves. Many children seem to have a natural tendency to start both letters and numerals from the bottom.

2. Quick handwriting is an aid to good spelling: poor handwriting is a positive hindrance.

3. Pride in well-presented work can be a powerful incentive. Conversely, embarrassment over poor presentation may inhibit the writer from producing more than a few lines.

Handwriting as a craft

There are many different styles of handwriting currently in use in schools, each with its own supporters. We have no intention in this section of stating a preference for one or another, as the same basic principles apply to teaching almost any style. For convenience, however, the letter forms referred to will be in the Marion Richardson style, which is used quite widely in our schools.

We view handwriting as a craft or skill which should be taught carefully from the beginning. Letter shapes developed haphazardly by children are usually incorrect, and become impossible to eradicate once they are well established. Creativity in writing should be restricted to the content and structure of the theme, and not be allowed to extend as far as the letter forms. Once children have mastered a basic style, they will naturally wish to develop their own version of it. If the original learning has been sound, further experiments in style are likely to remain legible and speedy.

Handwriting skill is therefore entirely different from reading and spelling; it can, without detriment, be learned through drills. It is better practised, not when the writer's urge to put down ideas is pressing, but as a separate skill, much as a learner driver may practise changing gears in the garage with the engine switched off before attempting to drive on a busy road. A further difference from other language-related skills is that handwriting can be taught successfully to quite large groups, provided that the teacher does frequent tours of the classroom to ensure that everyone is making the correct hand movements.

Script or cursive?

A common pattern of development in a child's handwriting goes as follows:

1. The child makes random-looking attempts to copy print or the teacher's script.

2. The teacher shows the child how letters are to be formed. There are two major ways of doing this. One is to emphasize the constituent shapes of the letter, e.g. 'a stick and then a ball' for 'b'. A better way is to verbalize the movements required to form the letter, e.g. 'down then up and round in a circle' for 'b'.

3. As a result children learn to write
    either in their own haphazard style
    or in the teacher's analytical 'constituent shapes' style
    or in the teacher's 'continuous movement' style, which can be the foundation for cursive writing.

4. At a later stage, anywhere between Junior One and Junior Four, the child learns a cursive style of handwriting from class lessons on the blackboard or from published cards.

There are many points along this developmental pathway at which the child can begin to acquire those faulty writing habits which result in poor handwriting. We believe that here, as in other aspects of education, prevention is better than cure. In cases where poor habits have been established, however, it is usually assumed that a correct form of script should be learned before a cursive style is adopted. This may be advisable at the infant level, but there is a strong case for carefully structured teaching of cursive writing to all pupils at Junior One stage, especially if the standard of script writing is poor. The reason for this is that it is easier to acquire a set of new prestigious habits than to correct established ones.

When children have learned a cursive style, with poor results, it is still preferable to teach them either the same or a different cursive style, rather than revert to script. With practice, the flow and rhythm of the cursive styles take over from previous wrong forms.

Stages in the development of handwriting

Stage One: Pencil control

At the end of this stage the child performs consistently the following:

1. Holds the pencil in a relaxed and natural grip which allows the writer to read what has just been written. (Some allowance may have to be made for individual preferences here.)

2. Makes writing movements from left to right across the page in lines from top to bottom of the page.

3. Has sufficient pencil control to trace simple rhythmic patterns in continuous lines.

4. Copies such patterns satisfactorily.

5. Identifies and refers to letters by name or sound.

6. Follows handwriting instructions, e.g. 'start at the top'; 'a tail with a curl'.

Stage Two: Reproducing letter shapes

At the end of this stage the child performs consistently the following tasks:

1. Writes the correct form of all letters, possibly whilst repeating verbal instructions (e.g. **n** is a short stick then over the bridge).

2. Classifies letters by the writing movement required, (e.g. all these begin with a

    c : a, c, d, g, o, q

3. Writes letters of an even, appropriate size.

4. Spaces letters and words correctly.

5. In cursive writing, knows the joins that go with each letter (e.g. **o, w, r,** and **v** are 'top-joiners' as distinct from 'bottom-joiners' **a, m, n,** and **u**). Compare

    bog, bag; bark, bank

6. Knows the effect of 'top-joiners' on the letter that follows. Compare

    de, be ; ds, bs

Stage Three: Fluent writing

At the end of this stage the child uses her handwriting skill as a tool without conscious thought about its operation.

Handwriting activities and materials

As the above tabulation of development of handwriting illustrates, poor handwriting may be the result of inadequate learning about letter-shapes and joins, or of insufficient skill in controlling the pencil, or both.

The fine co-ordination of small muscular movements in the hand, which gives good pencil control, develops at different rates in different individuals. Many of the activities provided in infant schools are designed to enable children to practise and refine these movements. General clumsiness and confusion over the left-to-right direction of writing often accompany specific reading difficulties. The teacher may feel unsure where to begin to teach.

As with reading, it is advisable to begin with one or two targets, and a variety of activities. The nature of the targets and the purpose of the activities should be made clear to children, so that they can consciously direct their efforts to the same end. Where possible, suggestions about the ways of learning should come from the children themselves, for example:

Teacher: 'How are you going to remember which way round b goes, Robin?'

Robin: 'I can look at the b in the middle of my name.'

Patterns and movements in a variety of media should help children to gain control of their hand muscles. Most children enjoy using poster paint, thick crayons, and chalk. A cautionary note should, however, be sounded here. If the purpose of the exercise is to improve handwriting skill, all movements must be from left to right, and they should be rhythmic and continuous. Furthermore, there is no guarantee that large movements practised with thick implements will transfer to pencil and paper. In the first place, the grip for holding a pencil is more complicated than that for holding chalk.

A further matter for consideration is the position of the source from which the child is copying. The best position for the writing card or teacher's writing is immediately above the child's writing paper. If the original is placed to the right or the left, the child may copy mirror-wise. And even greater difficulties arise when copying from a blackboard. Here the task requires the child to transfer:

1.   White writing on black to black on white.

2.   Large shapes to small shapes.

3.   From several feet away to only inches away.

4.   From a vertical plane to a much smaller horizontal plane, probably of a different shape.

If the child is not seated facing the blackboard, but sideways on or even facing away from it, the task becomes more difficult. Whenever possible, give children with such difficulties work cards instead.

Writing materials

The materials with which the child works should also be given some thought. Tracing paper, for example, is not satisfactory for children with pencil control problems, especially when the reproduction is not clear, or where there is insufficient contrast between print and paper. Since Stage One is concerned with pencil control, materials here should be evaluated carefully for clarity and size. At Stage Two, when letter shapes are to be learned, models for copying must be clear and unambiguous.

Choice of writing paper for practice and for written work is influenced by many factors. Infant teachers, for example, often prefer unlined paper because young children find it easier to use. Keeping the writing on the lines is too demanding for them when they have to concentrate also on letter shape, size and spacing. As a result, many infants learn to keep their lines of writing straight and well-shaped, although they may write letters like p, g and y with their tails on rather than below the line.

The purpose of using lined paper is to help the writer present the work well. If children find lines difficult to manage, or a particular spacing inappropriate to the size of their writing, then they should see if blank paper or a different spacing suits them better. In the story written by Richard which is reproduced in the section on 'spelling', for example, the lines on the paper are too narrow for his size of handwriting. Care should be taken not to suggest that one kind of paper is more 'babyish' or 'grown-up' than another. If children are allowed to participate in the decision about what kind of writing paper suits them individually, they can then be expected to make efforts to improve their writing.

For handwriting practice and letter formation many teachers use special double-lined exercise books in which lower-case letters must be written touching top and bottom lines. Some children find these very difficult to use, either because their handwriting is bigger or smaller than the space, or because there are too many variables to attend to at the same time. The teacher should watch the child's attempts at using the book and decide what is causing the problem. Does he need to give all his attention to the letter shapes? Is his pencil control sufficient to allow him to touch the top line? He might make better progress with a different ruling or even need paper with lines drawn by the teacher.

Spacing

Some children have difficulty in leaving suitable spaces between words in their writing. The solution to the problem lies first in making the child aware of the function of spaces, that is, that they make reading easier. Children sometimes use the little finger of their non-writing hand as a measure of space between words, but this can prove difficult for the child who has poor control of writing anyway. We may have to accept that in some cases spacing must take a low priority, and that children cannot be expected to give their attention to all aspects of handwriting and to spelling and content simultaneously.

Left-handedness

Left-handers have difficulty with handwriting because the movements required have been developed by right-handers. The natural inclination is to write in an outward direction from the body, which would result in left-handers writing mirror-wise. The teacher who is aware of the problems can ensure that the left-hander is helped as much as possible by paying attention to the following points.

1. Position

The writing hand should not be next to another child's writing hand, and so a left-hander should sit on the left not on the right of a right-hander. Since the writing hand is moving towards the body rather than away from it, the left-hander also needs to be distanced from the writing paper by sitting in the right-hand half of his own desk. These points are illustrated in the diagram below.

2. Movement

Whereas the right-hander draws the pen along, the left-hander pushes his. Consequently, the left-hander digs the nib into the paper, smudges his work, and covers up what has just been written. It has been found helpful if the writing-paper is positioned at an angle (see diagram). Left-handed nibs or roller ball pens are usually easier to control than fine nibs.

3. Pen grip

Left-handers need to hold the pen slightly higher up the shaft than right-handers. Some left-handers develop a 'crook' grip with the hand above the writing. If the resulting handwriting is badly formed, slow, or in other ways inefficient, the teacher may find it worthwhile to attempt to correct this habit, but should be aware that the child will find it difficult and must be convinced that the change is worth the considerable effort required.

4. Self-image

In the past, left-handers have been teased or even reviled for their oddity, and there is still a trace of such attitudes in some areas. Discretion in making special arrangements for left-handers will make them feel less different. It should not appear that left-handers are being given extra concessions.

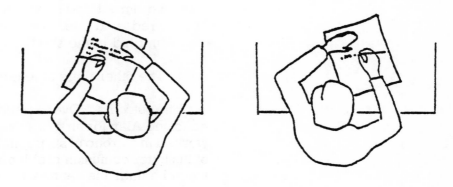

Case studies

The following examples illustrate the importance of limited targets, good models and, most of all, the child's own motivation.

Case study 1: Alan

(The account is written by his teacher)

Alan's main problem is not his reading but his writing. He confuses b/d, h/n, a/u, and consistently writes capital B and D because he is obviously unsure which way they should be written. He holds his pencil correctly, but many of his letters are formed incorrectly which is possibly one cause of his confusion.

I decided to begin with b/d confusion, and to teach the correct cursive form of only one of these, the letter d, because it is made with an easier continuous movement than b. I thought it important to teach d in isolation from the letter b, to avoid further confusion. Once d was firmly grasped as part of the letter family formed in this way (a, c, d, g, o, q), the formation of b could be learned separately. The approach I used was then adapted to each letter pair causing confusion. This was the teaching sequence I followed:

1. Establish that Alan hears the difference between the two letters in speech and pronounces them distinctly. This should be no problem with b/d but may be a factor in a/u.

2. Show how to form the letter slowly and carefully, say, in a sandtray, then more quickly and fluently with finger

paint or a dry finger on a dusty blackboard, covering the blackboard with <u>d</u>'s written quickly and accurately. Then use pencil and lined paper and practise until fluency and appropriate size are established. Each time he writes it, Alan should repeat the sound <u>d</u>.

3.   Since one or two other children in the class sometimes confuse <u>b</u> and <u>d</u>, provide a reference point for all of them by sticking a large letter <u>d</u> to the classroom door.

4.   'Language in Action' books (Macmillan) have a felt letter shape on the front which can be traced forming the letter correctly. Alan enjoyed reading the story with me and listening and looking for the <u>d</u> sounds.

5.   Alan made up his own story for the letter <u>d</u> with some help. It read: 'One day Fred the dog was digging in the garden. He dug and dug until he had a deep hole. Then he buried dad's red slipper in it. What have you done Fred, said dad. You have dug up my daisies. Fred ran and hid in the shed.'

6.   The other pairs of letters were taught in a similar way.

The outcome: Over a period of eight weeks, I have managed to see Alan for an extra five minutes most days and he has worked in a group of six pupils for half an hour each day. Most of his letter confusion problems have been overcome, except when he finds the set task too difficult. Then he concentrates on the content and cannot give as much attention to the writing. He is continuing to practise fluent letter formation with the rest of the class and, as his cursive writing style improves, the formation of all letters should become entirely automatic.

Case study 2:   Karen

Karen, aged nine, moved to her present school at the end of the second year in Junior School. All other members of her class had by then received instruction in cursive handwriting. Karen developed her own individual version. She was an avid reader and enjoyed writing long stories, although no one else could read them! She confused b/d, p/q, no/on. Her teacher, mother and Karen herself worked out a programme to be followed at school and at home.

Stage One: Pencil control

1.   Karen grips the pencil very tightly, too near the point. A triangular plastic pencil grip helps her to adopt a more conventional hold. Vinyl pencil grips are not expensive and can be obtained from 'Living and Learning' Duke Street, Wisbech, Cambs, PE13 2AE.
   She sits with her feet on the chair-rung, left hand shielding her book, head six inches away from the page at an angle, tongue protruding. We agree that she should start each writing session with both feet on the floor, left hand steadying the exercise book, and head up. This is referred to as 'posture'.

2.   Karen's left-to-right movement is satisfactory.

3. Karen copies patterns satisfactorily.

4. Letter names. Karen calls y <u>you</u> and u <u>yer.</u> This is easily solved by practising spelling out by letter names words containing one or both letters. This is not a spelling test and the words are displayed in front of Karen as she spells them aloud.

5. Following instructions: Karen does not always understand what is required and needs one-to-one supervision so that she may learn the conventional instructions.

Stage Two: Reproducing letter shapes

Karen does not know about correct letter formations; the items she performs correctly seem to work by chance and not according to system. We decide that she should learn first the shapes and joins of letters based on c, because the letters are distinctive, (i.e. a, c, d, g, o, q).

Each letter has its own instructions, to be verbalized, for example:

(i) start at the top and round to the line and up to join the next letter (c).

(ii) start at the top and round to the line. Close the circle and give it a tail (g).

Letters are practised in isolation and in short combinations e.g. dad, dog, cog. Some nonsense syllables are included in order to emphasize the different joins for ag and og.

Karen arranges to practise the week's work, taken from the Marion Richardson handwriting scheme, under her mother's supervision for 10 minutes each school day evening. The aim is to provide adequate regular practice without fatigue, and to ensure that only correct forms are used. Copying exercises are provided, and every session must begin with correct posture.

Meanwhile, Karen is advised to revert to her former script style for classroom use, despite the fact that she forms every letter incorrectly from the bottom up. It is considered preferable for her to have two styles of writing, even though one is incorrect, until she has mastered the new cursive style correctly, to avoid the contamination of wrong habits.

As she practises each set of letter shapes, Karen ticks them off on an alphabet chart. Each tick represents 5 × 10 minute sessions. The teacher tests each week's work by dictating words to be written. Success is praised. Errors are corrected by Karen with the reminder, 'Tell yourself the instructions for writing it'.

The criterion for mastery is that every letter is written correctly in a dictation of 20 words including each letter at least 5 times. Any letter not mastered receives further practice the following week. Karen and her teacher complete together the 'Handwriting Record' reproduced in Table 10.2.

Table 10.1:
Letter formation

c shapes	*a, c, d, g*
n shapes	*h, m, n, p*
l shapes	*i, l, t, u, v, w, y*
oddities	*b, e, f, j, k, r, s, x, 3*
tall letters	*b, d, f, h, l, t*
tails below	*f, g, j, p, q, y, 3*
top joiners	*b, f, o, r, v, w*

As each group is practised, letters already learned are naturally incorporated into the work, and the range of words increased.

At the end of eight weeks Karen can copy accurately and fairly quickly and the appearance of her writing is pleasing. She is now permitted to use her new skill for class work, on the understanding that she checks through it for handwriting errors with her teacher or her mother and practises corrections. Despite careful teaching, she confuses <u>b</u> and <u>d</u>. She therefore has the additional task of checking through her work and awarding herself a small tick for every <u>b</u> written correctly. Ten ticks earn a star for the front cover of her story book.

Karen has now embarked on a structured spelling programme. She recognizes the importance of correct handwriting in helping her to spell.

Comment

Karen had strong personal motivation for wanting to write correctly, and she was willing to work. Her mother was supportive, and recognized the value of praise for achieving small steps of progress.

Cursive handwriting is not difficult to learn once it has been broken down into simple tasks. For young children it has enormous prestige as a 'grown up' activity. The wise teacher takes advantage of this natural motivation to encourage her children to develop a good legible style.

Table 10.2:
Handwriting record

CODE: 1. Copies 2. Writes from dictation 3. Correct in free writing

Set 1: c-shapes Set 2: n-shapes Set 3: l-shapes Set 4: Oddities

a ☐	h ☐	i ☐	b ☐
c ☐	m ☐	l ☐	e ☐
d ☐	n ☐	t ☐	f ☐
g ☐	r ☐	u ☐	j ☐
o ☐		v ☐	k ☐
q ☐		w ☐	r ☐
		y ☐	s ☐
			x ☐
			3 ☐

Joins

	Bottom joins	Top joins
c-shapes	☐	☐
n-shapes	☐	☐
l-shapes	☐	☐
Oddities	☐	☐

Chapter 11   More suggestions for parents

Parents are teachers

Throughout the manual we have referred to the central role parents can play in co-operation with the teacher. To start with, parents can tell teachers a great deal about their children, for instance, how they learn best, what motivates them, or any particular difficulties they have experienced.

Usually, on reaching school, the child will have acquired the language and cognitive skills needed to begin to learn to read. If nursery rhymes, songs and stories have been read in the security of the home, these activities will have prepared the child for learning at school. The parents of the child with reading difficulties have often done the important ground work. The child enjoys stories and talks with interest and understanding about them. Although there may be some difficulties with the automatic aspects of deciphering the printed text, the child's language skills can become invaluable in compensating for such difficulties.

It is particularly important that parents continue to read aloud stories and information which the child wants to hear. This will keep the interest in books alive. It will also develop the child's knowledge so that it is possible to keep up with those who have had the good fortune to learn to read easily.

Working with parents

In Chapter Two we described the disappointment and anxiety felt by the pupil, the parents and the teacher alike when there are difficulties with learning to read. These feelings can easily lead to an expectation of failure, so that learning becomes even harder. Our ability to acquire any complex skill is adversely affected by worry and anxiety. It is essential, therefore, to plan the learning programme in such a way as to sustain the pupil's confidence that he or she will eventually succeed in learning to read, write and spell.

Setting clear, limited and attainable targets, and recording their successful achievement, allows the pupil to feel in control of the learning process. These feelings of control are a good antidote to learning anxiety. Such a programme also permits the pupil to practise at home with the help of parents, so long as they know what is required and understand the importance of a positive and encouraging approach. If a child has learning difficulties, we can't just send a book home to be read. Teachers must explain carefully to the pupil and the parent how the home practice sessions should be carried out, and what the parents can do to ensure the best chance of success. The detailed suggestions provided in the previous chapters of this manual will help you tailor your approach to the needs of the individual pupil. They have been written in such a way that certain sections, particularly those in a step-by-step form, can be followed by parents in the home practice periods.

Chapter Five, 'Rehearsal and repetition', contains advice

that is particularly useful for parents. It emphasizes the importance of choosing reading books which are 'easy', and then preparing the reading practice in a way that maintains the pupil's confidence. This may, for example, involve repeated reading of the same book. That is, the book is first *read to* the pupil; then, in later readings, the pupil gradually takes over more and more of the independent reading. This approach may well contrast with the pupil's and parents' expectations of 'page-by-page' reading practice. It is therefore vitally important to explain to parents and pupils that there is a need for greater repetition in order to ensure pleasurable 'success-orientated' practice, with the emphasis on the content and the language of the book.

Fluency and enjoyment in reading should be the aim rather than the collection of books as 'scalps' that have been laboriously acquired, page by page, with little appreciation for the story as a whole. In order to follow this approach, the school's stock of books needs to contain a good selection of short, interesting and easily read books. Publications such as NARE A-Z Reading List (Atkinson and Gains 1983; see Resources page at the end of the manual) classify books according to their reading levels. Local reading centres and school library services usually have an ample selection of suitable books on display.

Teamwork between parent, pupil and teacher can be very rewarding if an atmosphere of mutual support is established, and everyone appreciates and acknowledges the efforts made by other members of the team. This is not as easy as it sounds. Regular meetings make heavy demands on time for both parents and teachers. A few parents may have good reasons for not wanting to participate in teaching. They may feel that they are unable to remain calm and encouraging when helping their own children. This can be a familiar experience for teachers too, who have enormous patience when helping other people's children but are on a 'short fuse' when teaching their own. This is only natural. Our concern for our own children is so great that we become too involved in their difficulties. If parents realize that their feelings of irritation and frustration are only natural consequences of their concern, and if the learning tasks are designed to promote rather than thwart a sense of achievement, then most parents are capable of playing a vital role in the teaching process.

Projects of parental involvement

Our definition of reading in Chapter One assumes that the reader utilises simultaneously information from several sources: visual information, phonic information, information about grammar and about meaning. When the pupil has difficulty in one of these areas, other areas can to some extent compensate for it. Therefore, different children learn to read in different ways according to their particular cognitive and perceptual strengths and weaknesses.

If we do not know in what way the pupil is going to learn to read, our simplest course of action is just to provide enjoyable opportunities for learning. The analogy of acquiring skills of swimming has been used to illustrate this. We do not know how the child combines the various movements involved in staying afloat. The many 'styles' of swimming the first length bears witness to the diversity of ways in which children can learn. The one certain thing is that the more often we take the child to the swimming pool for happy confidence building play and practice, the more likely it is that the child will learn to swim. Recent projects of parental participation in the teaching of reading have been based on this principle. Parents have received guidance in how to read with their children regularly and the school has helped in the choice of appropriate books. The teaching of subskills such as phonics has been avoided.

A large number of projects have demonstrated the effectiveness of parents as partners in the teaching of reading. They have involved children throughout the primary school age range and have included schools in multicultural areas. Often other members of the family, such as older siblings, have become involved as helpers. A few projects report success with older pupils, for example, Sixth Formers have followed the 'paired reading' procedure described below with either younger pupils in their own schools or with pupils in a neighbouring primary school. The book *Parental Involvement in Children's Reading*, edited by Keith Topping and Sheila Wolfendale (1985), presents a useful review of current practice and gives details of a wide range of local schemes.

All the reading projects have certain common elements which we shall enumerate here:

1. Regular contact with parents. Some of the projects have involved home visits by teachers or researchers at fortnightly or less frequent intervals. Others have arranged meetings at school, seeing parents individually or as a group, at the beginning and end of a limited project time lasting some six to eight weeks. If parents have not been able to attend the initial meeting at school, teachers have been willing to visit them at home to explain the project.

2. Attractively illustrated guides have been explained in detail during the initial meetings. Such guides are currently available, as part of information packs and demonstration videotapes for schools, from the teachers' centres of many local education authorities such as ILEA, Kirklees and Cleveland. The guidelines have placed particular emphasis on praise and encouragement. Table 11.1 gives an example of the advice to parents given in a school in Stockport. The layout originates from the Belfield Project (Jackson and Hannon, 1981).

3. Parents have been asked to read with their child most evenings for a short time, ranging from 5 minutes to 20 minutes each session.

4. A daily record with space for comments by both teachers and parents has ensured that close contact between school and home has been maintained.

5. Many schools have provided special folders for the reading project which have both protected the books and given the project high status.

Paired or shared reading

The terms 'paired reading' and 'shared reading' have been used in a similar way to describe techniques which consist of the parent and the child reading aloud together from a book of the child's choice. They read in chorus and the parent, or other helper, does not stop to pay attention to the child's mistakes. They continue to read together, the parent or the child pointing at each word as it is read, even when the child can manage only a few of the words in the text. The parent adjusts the pace of reading to suit the child.

Shared reading can be seen as a transitional stage between hearing a story read aloud and becoming an independent reader. The parent provides an instant model while the child's attention is focused on the printed word. The child is actively involved and learns incidentally about the stresses and rhythms of reading, about punctuation and about reading for meaning. The technique provides children with the opportunity to enjoy any books which interest them, even those which would otherwise be too difficult for them.

Paired reading involves two sets of instructions. In the first, reading together, the parent and the child read each word aloud together. They usually read quite slowly. If the child struggles and hesitates for more than five seconds with a particular word, the parent says the word, and the child repeats it after the parent and reading in chorus then continues. The second set of instructions is followed when the text is so easy that the child can read sections independently. Then the child signals to the parent to remain quiet (e.g. by knocking on the table) and reads alone until a difficult word is encountered. The parent again models the word for the child and they continue to read together until the child feels ready to read alone.

The techniques of shared or paired reading are described in detail in the publications mentioned above. It is important that teachers and parents adapt the methods to suit the needs of individual children.

Helping children with specific learning difficulties

A project described by Young and Tyre (1983) involved a group of children aged between 8 and 13, who had been identified by recognized 'specialists' as having specific learning difficulties in reading/spelling. The children were given intensive help, primarily by their parents, over a period of one year. At the end of the year the children had made gains in Reading Age ranging from 1 year to 3 years.

The parents attended a day course and a teacher-researcher visited them at home at regular intervals. The children were taught by their parents for 30 minutes per day.

Initially, the children were given books which were some two years below their level of reading ability. Table 11.2 gives a brief outline of the teaching methods followed during reading practice. Reading practice took 15 minutes. For the other 15 minutes the parents used the passages the children had read to play word games and to follow other prescribed activities. In this way reading went hand in hand with writing and spelling practice.

Conclusion

Children with reading difficulties will not suddenly make miraculous progress as a result of a short reading project. Limited projects can be used as a starting point to harness resources but, in order to make lasting gains, the children will need to receive help over a longer period of time.

We are not suggesting that the teacher should abdicate from the responsibility for progress in reading. Involving parents in helping their child read makes significant demands on time for both parents and teachers and requires careful preparation. To make the co-operation between teachers, parents and the child effective, the following conditions must be met:

- We need to adopt a positive and encouraging approach.
- We must provide clear guidelines of the teaching procedures which include a time limit for each task.
- Prospect of success should be evident.
- Regular opportunities for discussion and feedback should be arranged.
- Techniques of paired or shared reading should be adapted to suit the individual.
- Teachers and parents also need praise and encouragement.

Table 11.1:
Guidelines for parents

We hope you will enjoy the reading project. These notes are to help you remember what we discussed at the meeting.

Do:

1. Make sure the atmosphere is happy and relaxed.
2. Find a quiet place where there are no distractions.'
3. Sit down together so that both can see the book.
4. Talk about the book and about any illustrations first.
5. Talk about what has happened and what might happen next.
6. Smooth out any difficulties by reading any words your child doesn't know.
7. Talk about what you have read. If possible relate events in the story to the child's own experience.
8. Give lots of praise for effort.

Don't:

1. Make reading an unpleasant task.
2. Threaten to tell the teacher if the reading is not done.
3. Make the child think there is competition with someone else.
4. Show anxiety about lack of interest.
5. Ask the child to spell out or build up any words.
6. Get cross if you have to keep on helping with the same word.
7. Be afraid to ask for help and advice from any of the teachers, however trivial you feel the trouble is.

Table 11.2:
Daily reading practice – 15 minutes

1. Talk about the pictures, the characters and the story so far for two or three minutes.

2. Read the passage aloud with as much expression as possible, while running a finger along the line of print, for three minutes.

3. Read the passage aloud with the child joining in, in chorus, for three minutes. The child only needs to attempt to read each word.

4. Read the passage aloud again together, but this time pause occasionally for the child to provide the next word or phrase at points in the text when you feel reasonably certain that the child will be able to carry on – three minutes.

5. The child reads the passage aloud. If he hesitates, supply the word or phrase – three minutes.

6. Praise the child for joining in, for reading with expression, for supplying the right word, and for effort.

Adapted from Young and Tyre, 1983

Chapter 12 Conclusion

Getting the balance right

Throughout the text, the rationales for particular teaching methods have been illustrated with various analogies. It would be helpful at this point to remind you of what these were:

1. Some children may have particular difficulty with visual and phonic information, i.e. they cannot easily acquire the skills of recognizing letters, letter sounds and words. As we regard these as automatic skills (similar to driving a car or playing a musical instrument well), pupils with difficulty will need much extra practice to reach the point of automatic mastery. (From page 2.)

2. Learning to read may be likened to climbing a mountain; there are several possible routes to the top. Some learners need to take a slow and laborious route while others, more fortunate, can take the quickest one. Our task is to guide the learner along the route which we think suits him best. We want to make the journey as natural and as enjoyable as possible and should aim to help him pick up reading without artificial drills whenever possible. (From page 22.)

3. Learning to read is like learning to swim. We do not know how the child combines the various movements involved in staying afloat. The many 'styles' of swimming the first length bear witness to the diversity of ways in which children can learn. The one certain thing is that the more often we take the child to the swimming pool for happy, confidence building play and practice, the more likely it is that the child will learn to swim. (From page 103.)

All three analogies share an emphasis on ensuring that the learner approaches reading or writing in the knowledge that she *can* succeed. The importance of creating a relaxed atmosphere which enhances motivation and confidence cannot be stressed enough.

The analogies differ, however, with regard to the teaching methods they illustrate. Whilst at one extreme we have a structured, highly repetitive approach, including phonic drill when necessary, the other extreme favours plenty of interactive language-based reading practice where the teacher/parent is prepared to read for the child. Which method are we to follow? Ideally, the answer should be 'both', but with limited teaching time it is usually necessary to decide on priorities. Therefore, the answer depends on the judgement of the teacher and the needs of the individual child.

Referring back to Table 4.1 on page 14, the pupil who struggles with visual word recognition or phonics whilst use of meaning and context is good, can be considered to need more repetitive emphasis on sight words and appropriate phonics. Conversely, the child who 'barks at print' should be helped to read for meaning and have more of the text read for him. We have to get the balance right. Over-reliance on syntactic cues while ignoring phonic information will produce inaccurate reading. Too much emphasis on phonic cues with little attention to the syntax and meaning of the text ignores the very purpose of reading. The link between phonics and meaning can be illustrated with the following list of words:

mint
hint
flint
pint

If you have attended to phonics only, you will not have made sense of the last word in this list.

But, it is not enough to identify the child's areas of weakness and give him plenty of practice in those areas alone. We must also build on his strengths. It should be remembered that language cues, automatic visual memory and phonics are considered interdependent in the process of learning to read. If the pupil experiences difficulty in one area, the other areas may to some extent compensate for that weakness. For example, contextual cues and phonics may help the pupil who struggles with the visual aspects of word recognition.

There are not only slow or fast routes to competent and pleasurable reading; there are many kinds of routes or combinations of routes which depend on the make-up of the individual child. If it is recognized that different children learn to read in different ways according to their particular combinations of strengths and weaknesses, the teacher will not over-emphasize any one area of learning but build on a broad front. The case study of Peter below will illustrate the need for 'systematic flexibility'.

The suggestions we have made in the previous chapters have stressed the many ways of moving forward. We have given examples such as 'he had fish and ch... for dinner' where the pupil is encouraged to use both context and initial letters as cues. At the same time, we have provided opportunities for an increased rate of repetition, even in interactive reading, as described in Chapter 11.

The class teacher's dilemma

The Warnock Report (DES, 1978) and the 1981 Education Act imply that all teachers have responsibility for pupils with reading and writing difficulties. But how can the busy teacher, in charge of at least 30 children, find time to follow the suggestions made in this manual?

Teachers have attempted to solve the problem in a number of ways. In some schools, overall policy has favoured opportunities for individual work so that arrangements have been made to free each class teacher in turn to do their own remedial work. Joining up two classes for story time so that one of the teachers can work with a few children has worked quite well, but organizing the class so that all but a few are occupied with activities they can complete independently has not been easily achieved.

We are aware of the considerable pressures on the class teacher in the Primary School. However, when we have apologized to teachers for the demands on time made by our suggestions, we have been encouraged by the comment that knowing what to do makes it easier to find the time for doing it. In addition, many teachers have said that the extra reading/writing activities can be incorporated into the day's class activities so that the pupil with difficulties works at an appropriate level for a large part of the day. Isolated remedial help cannot achieve that kind of transfer into other aspects of the school work. In certain cases, two pupils have been able to work together, each in turn checking on the other's progress, for example, in individual spelling practice.

The teacher who can give the child with difficulties a maximum of five minutes of individual attention per day needs to decide about priorities. The case study of Peter below demonstrates how priorities were switched during one school year in response to the progress Peter was making.

A case study of Peter

1.   Background

Peter had started the second year in his Junior School with very little reliable knowledge of reading. On standardized tests he could identify a few words or phrases but his responses seemed due more to luck than real reading. Although Peter was disorganized and forgetful about practical matters, he did not seem unintelligent and knew a great deal about such subjects as gardening and wild life. Peter was no trouble in the class. He could copy the writing from books neatly and draw good illustrations, but he could not read what he had written. His teachers and parents were puzzled and worried.

2.   Assessment based on Table 4.1 (page 14)

Table 12.1 shows the progress Peter has made over the school year.

Table 12.1:
Assessing Peter's progress

At the beginning of the school year:		
CONCEPTS AND APPROACHES	**VISUAL RECOGNITION**	**PHONICS**
Stage II But Peter does not reliably attend to initial letter cues. He makes guesses based on context only and expects his teacher to stop him and correct him. Peter just wants to get it done.	Beginning of Stage II Peter reads very few words fluently but has no difficulty with Stage I tasks.	Stage II Peter knows most of the single letter sounds. In isolation he can blend consonant – vowel – consonant words but does not use this skill when reading a text.
At the end of the school year:		
Stage III Peter has become particularly good at self-correction. He re-reads if the text does not make sense. Peter also uses initial letters and consonant blends as cues, but when tired he tends to revert to guesses based on context alone.	Beginning of Stage III Peter has mastered well over 100 sight words but his automatic sight vocabulary is still very limited. He compensates with phonics and context.	Stage III Peter can read and spell his 'cards' (page 69). The cards are kept visible when he reads a text, to assist in transferring the knowledge to real reading.

3. Strengths and weaknesses

At the beginning of the school year:

(a) *Strengths*: Peter has mastered all the skills at Stage I. He talks intelligently about the story content and examines picture cues in great detail. His use of contextual cues is so good that it has over shadowed the other reading strategies to the point of becoming a drawback.

(b) *Weaknesses*: Peter has a despondent and over-dependant attitude to reading. He seems not to care whether his own guesses are right and relies on teacher corrections to make sense of the text. His most marked weakness appears to be in the area of visual word recognition while his use of phonics is so laborious that it does not readily transfer to reading a continuous text.

At the end of the school year:

(a) *Strengths*: Peter has a more confident attitude to reading and has become good at working out the sense of the story for himself (as long as the reading level is right). Use of contextual and syntactic cues is by far his strongest reading strategy.

(b) *Weaknesses*:   Although he has made good progress, Peter continues to need a very high rate of repetition before the recognition of a new word becomes automatic. Similarly, although Peter has learnt his phonic flipcards (page 69), his use of phonics when reading a text remains laborious. Peter has to concentrate intensely in order to combine all skills of reading. If there are distractions he relies only on contextual cues.

Comment: It can be seen that Peter is learning strategies to overcome or circumvent his difficulties in automatic visual memory and phonics. Although he still has a long way to go, he knows that he is making progress. It is, however, important to inform the Literacy Support Service or the Educational Psychology Service of Peter's problems as he is likely to have persistent difficulties, particularly with spelling.

4. What Peter's teacher did

Peter, his teacher and mother met and agreed to work together. Peter and his mother would work for 15 minutes most evenings. Notes in a reading exercise book (not on a card) would give instructions about what to practise and comment on how Peter was getting on. Further meetings were held approximately once a fortnight while the other pupils attended school assembly. On the whole this arrangement worked out well, although there were times when contact was not maintained or Peter became discouraged.

Autumn Term: It was decided to concentrate on massed practice of the reading vocabulary related to the pre-readers of a well-known reading scheme. Each book was read repeatedly following the instructions in Table 11.2, page 107. However, this did not encourage Peter to look and listen to words carefully. Therefore, Peter's teacher wrote key words on individual cards and Peter practised these cards following the suggestions mentioned in the case study of James (Chapter Six). The sight words were also used for spelling practice as described in Chapter Nine, because it was felt that learning to read and write the same words would help Peter. Phonics were introduced when words illustrating particular consonant blends or common digraphs appeared in the text. In this way, Peter started to build up his own pack of phonic flipcards as described on page 69.

His teacher spent the daily five minutes allocated to Peter checking over the work done at home and writing further instructions in the reading exercise book. Obviously, Peter's progress would have been much slower without his mother's help. In the classroom, written activities, as described in Chapter Five, were used to reinforce the reading practice.

By the Christmas holiday, Peter had drawn up a graph which indicated that he had mastered 80 new sight words. Over the holiday, Peter held a competition between the books he had read during the Autumn Term. The winner of the competition was the book which had been re-read most times.

Spring Term: Peter now moved on to the main reading books of the scheme. The procedure of repeated readings was again followed. Certain changes were made – the novelty of graphing sight words had worn off and it was decided to discontinue the use of packs of sight word cards. Instead, written work based on words in the text would provide the high level of repetition needed. Peter's pack of phonic flipcards was growing; each day a few minutes were spent checking over some of the cards.

Summer Term: Peter had read all the beginning books of the reading scheme. He was starting to find the later books rather long and heavy going. A wider range of books was needed to provide new interest and to consolidate what had been learnt. Peter was ready to select his own books from the school reading library. The books were colour coded so that he could pick any book with a Reading Age of less than 7 years. Peter was encouraged to select 'easy' books which had amusing cartoon-like illustrations. Peter's mother continued to follow the instructions in Table 11.2 (page 107) but she modified the rate of repetition needed according to the level of difficulty of the particular book. If a story proved too long or too difficult, Peter's mother would finish it for him. Meanwhile, the words on the phonic flipcards were used as the basis for spelling practice.

Plan for the Autumn Term: Peter and his mother intend to maintain the interactive reading practice of easy books throughout the summer holiday. They have borrowed some books from school and have also found the local library a helpful source for further reading.

When Peter returns to school in September, it should be time to move to the next stage of the structured approach. This will involve massed practice of the middle sections of the reading scheme; written work and phonic drill will be related to the vocabularly of these books. Simultaneously, Peter will want to continue with free reading of a wide range of easier books.

5. Discussion

The case study of Peter has been offered not as an infallible recipe but as an illustration of the choices made by his teacher. Other 'routes' could also have resulted in good progress. While theoretical knowledge of the processes involved in reading remains incomplete, it is only natural that opinions should differ about methods of teaching. We must, however, not allow our doubts about the most appropriate methods to paralyse us into indecision. If that happens, the pupil will make no progress at all. In this manual we have stressed the following points:

1. Assessment based on Table 4.1 which provides a framework for intervention.
2. A learning programme which builds on all aspects of reading.
3. Links between reading and writing activities.
4. Mastery learning of key skills.
5. A flexible plan which recognizes that progress is not linear.
6. The importance of records to mark progress.
7. The value of teamwork between teacher, child and parents.
8. The crucial role played by an encouraging and confidence-building approach.

The right to read

'... there is no higher nationwide priority in the field of education than the provision of the right to read for all...'
(James E. Allen, U.S. Commissioner of Education, 1970)

Those living in the twentieth century who have not acquired a certain level of competence in literacy cannot live a full individual and social life. If they have not gained the ability to read in the course of early education, they lack the essential skill for all other areas of learning.

As reading and writing are a fundamental necessity in modern life, it is our duty as parents and teachers to do the utmost in ensuring that every child has sufficient opportunity to learn. The reading and language policy of a school should, therefore, recognize individual differences so that those who take longer to learn have the right to receive more individual help.

The 1981 Education Act makes all local education authorities, through their schools, responsible for identifying those pupils who may have special educational needs. When an individual pupil has followed the programme outlined in this manual for a period of time and continues to have marked and persistent difficulties, we advise you to contact your local Literacy Support Service or Educational Psychology Service. Your records of the systematic way in which you have attempted to help the child will provide an invaluable basis for further remedial action.

Bibliography

AINSCOW, M. and TWEDDLE, D.A. (1984). *Early Learning Skills Analysis*. Chichester: Wiley.

ALLEN, J.E. (1970). 'The Right to Read – Targets for the 70s'. In: MELNIK, A. and MERRITT, J. (Eds) *Reading Today and Tomorrow*. London: Hodder and Stoughton.

AMES, E. (1983). *Teach Yourself to Diagnose Reading Problems*. London: Macmillan Education.

ARNOLD, H. (1982). *Listening to Children Reading*. London: Hodder and Stoughton in association with the United Kingdom Reading Association.

BRADLEY, L. and BRYANT, P. (1983). 'Categorising sounds and learning to read: a causal connection', *Nature*, **301**, 419 – 21.

'Breakthrough to Literacy' series. Harlow: Longman.

CLAY, M. (1979). *The Early Detection of Reading Difficulties: a Diagnostic Survey with Recovery Procedures*. (2nd Edn.) Auckland, New Zealand: Heinemann.

CLAY, M. (1982). *Observing Young Readers*. London: Heinemann.

DEAN, J. and NICHOLSON, R. (1974). *Framework for Reading*. London: Evans.

GREAT BRITAIN. DEPARTMENT OF EDUCATION AND SCIENCE (1981). *Education Act 1981*. London: HMSO.

GREAT BRITAIN. DEPARTMENT OF EDUCATION AND SCIENCE (1978). *Special Educational Needs*. (The Warnock Report). London: HMSO.

GREENWOOD, G. (1978). 'Audiovisual Aids'. In: HINSON, M. (Ed) *Encouraging Results*. London: Macmillan.

HARING, N.G., LOVITT, T.C., EATON, M.D., HANSEN, C.L. (1980). *The Fourth R – Research in the Classroom*. Columbus, Ohio: Charles E. Merrill Publishing Company.

JACKSON, A. and HANNON, P. (1981). *The Belfield Reading Project*. Rochdale: Belfield Community Council.

JACKSON, S. (1971). *Get Reading Right*. Glasgow: Robert Gibson and Sons.

JEFFREE, D. and SKEFFINGTON, M. (1980). *Let Me Read*. London: Souvenir Press.

LAWRENCE, D. (1973). *Improving Reading Through Counselling*. London: Ward Lock.

McKENZIE, M. (1980). *Helping Your Child with Reading – Parents' Guide*. London: Franklin Watts.

PEARSON, L. and LINDSAY, G. (1986). *Special Needs in the Primary School: Identification and Intervention*. Windsor: NFER-NELSON.

PETERS, M.L. (1975). *Diagnostic and Remedial Spelling Manual*. London: Macmillan.

PETERS, M.L. (1985). *Spelling: Caught or Taught? A New Look*. London: Routledge and Kegan Paul.

PRESLAND, J.L. (1982). 'Applying psychology to teaching the three Rs, reading and written English', *Occasional Papers of the Division of Educational and Child Psychology of the British Psychological Society*, **6**, 1, 3 – 38.

PUMFREY, P.D. (1985). *Reading: Tests and Assessment Techniques*. (2nd Edn). London: Hodder and Stoughton.

REASON, R. (1986). 'Specific learning difficulties: the development and evaluation of an INSET manual on intervention', *Educational and Child Psychology*, **3**, 1, 45 – 58. Division of Educational and Child Psychology of the British Psychological Society.

SMITH, F. (1984). *Joining the Literacy Club*. Reading: Centre for the Teaching of Reading, University of Reading.

SOMERFIELD, M., TORBE, M., WARD, C. for Coventry LEA (1984). *A Framework for Reading: Creating a Policy in the Primary School*. Tadworth: Heinemann.

TANSLEY, P. and PANCKHURST, J. (1981). *Children with Specific Learning Difficulties*. Windsor: NFER-NELSON.

THATCHER, J. (1984). *Teaching Reading to Mentally Handicapped Children*. London: Croom Helm.

TOPPING, K. and WOLFENDALE, S. (Eds) (1985). *Parental Involvement in Children's Reading*. London: Croom Helm.

TORBE, M. (1977). *Teaching Spelling*. London: Ward Lock.

VINCENT, D. (1985). *Reading Tests in the Classroom: an Introduction*. Windsor: NFER-NELSON.

YOUNG, P. and TYRE, C. (1983). *Dyslexia or Illiteracy? Realizing the Right to Read*. Milton Keynes: Open University Press.

Resources

ATKINSON, E.J. and GAINS, C.W. (1985). *An A – Z of Reading Books*. National Association of Remedial Education, 2 Lichfield Road, Stafford ST17 4JX.

BAKER, P. and J. *Language and Reading Games*. London: Macmillan Educational.

CLARKE, H. (1980). *Two-Way Spelling*. London: E.J. Arnold.

COTTERELL, G. (1973). *Checklist of Basic Sounds*. In: COTTERELL, G. *Diagnosis in the Classroom*. Reading: Centre for the Teaching of Reading, University of Reading.

CUFF, C. and MACKAY, D. (1981). *Super Spell*. Harlow: Longman.

Games for Developing Reading Skills. National Association of Remedial Education, 2 Lichfield Road, Stafford ST17 4JX.

HERBERT, D. and DAVIES-JONES, G. (1983). *A Classroom Index of Phonic Resources*. National Association of Remedial Education, 2 Lichfield Road, Stafford ST17 4JX.

HORNSBY, B. and SHEAR, F. (1980). *Alpha to Omega*. London: Heinemann Educational Books.

JARMAN, C. (1979). *The Development of Handwriting*. Oxford: Basil Blackwell.

NICHOLSON, D. and WILLIAMS, G. (1975). *Word Games for the Teaching of Reading*. London: Pitman Educational.

RICHARDSON, M. *Handwriting and Writing Patterns*. London: University of London Press.

ROOT, B. *Family Pairs, More Family Pairs, I – Spy, Make-It, Match-It, Pair-It, Phonic Pairs, Phonic Sets*. 'Games' Series. London: Hart-Davis.

SOUTHGATE, V. and HAVENHAND, J. (1968). *Sounds and Words*. London: University of London Press.

Index